Exile through a Gendered Lens

Exile through a Gendered Lens

Women's Displacement in Recent European History, Literature, and Cinema

Edited by Gesa Zinn and
Maureen Tobin Stanley

First published in 2012 by PALGRAVE MACMILLAN® in the United States—a division of St. Martin's Press LLC, 175 Fifth Avenue, New York, NY 10010

Where this book is distributed in the UK, Europe and the rest of the world, this is by Palgrave Macmillan, a division of Macmillan Publishers Limited, registered in England, company number 785998, of Houndmills, Basingstoke, Hampshire RG21 6XS.

Palgrave Macmillan is the global academic imprint of the above companies and has companies and representatives throughout the world.

Palgrave® and Macmillan® are registered trademarks in the United States, the United Kingdom, Europe and other countries.

ISBN: 978-0-230-33999-6

Library of Congress Cataloging-in-Publication Data

Zinn, Gesa
    Exile through a gendered lens: women's displacement in recent European history, literature, and cinema / edited by Gesa Zinn and Maureen Tobin Stanley.
        p. cm.
    ISBN 978-0-230-33999-6
    1. Women and literature—Europe—History—20th century. 2. Exile writings. 3. Exiled women authors. 4. Literature and transnationalism. 5. Gender identity in literature. I. Zinn, Gesa. II. Tobin Stanley, Maureen.

PN471.E95 2012
809'.89287—dc23   2011039849

A catalogue record of the book is available from the British Library.

Design by Scribe Inc.

First edition: April 2012

10 9 8 7 6 5 4 3 2 1

Printed and bound in Great Britain by
CPI Antony Rowe, Chippenham and Eastbourne

For Mikaela, Saskia, and Michael
and for Elena, Gabriel, and Thomas

Contents

Acknowledgment

We wish to thank the College of Liberal Arts and the University of Minnesota Duluth for providing us with research opportunities and funding for our book project. We also wish to acknowledge all whose support has been instrumental in bringing this project to fruition.

Introduction

Gesa Zinn and Maureen Tobin Stanley

In this book we investigate and explore when and how women from diverse backgrounds, national origins, social classes, and ethnicities became and continue to be the incontrovertible other within twentieth- and twenty-first century history. Each of the chapters within this anthology problematizes, sheds light on, underscores, and subverts gendered otherness and alienhood. The condition of other is that of exclusion, of inferiority, yet also of inequality, prohibition from privilege and, at times, from rights.

The adjectival and nominal term "other"—which can be traced to the Sanskrit "antara"—connotes difference, distinction, or separation from that which is already mentioned, implied, or understood. Similarly, the term "alien," stemming from the Latin for "other," is quite similar in etymology, if not synonymous. An "other" and an "alien" as nouns are equivalents—at least in their language origins. Yet the term "alien" has permutated to include the following accepted concepts. As an adjective, "alien" can signify strange or unlike or dissimilar to one's own; adverse, hostile, or opposed. As a noun, it can connote the meaning of the adjective as applied to a person, place, or thing, and it can also refer to a resident of a host nation who, although having been born in his or her country of origin, has not acquired citizenship within the host nation an estranged or excluded individual, a foreigner, even an extraterrestrial, one who is not from this world, literally or figuratively. The antithesis, or the antonym perhaps, of an alien is a citizen—one who belongs to a geographic locus and is protected and granted rights by the government of that jurisdiction.

Yet if we think of gendered otherness for female citizens, we must acknowledge that women are a collective other when they—in spite of being citizens—continue to lack protection and rights under the hegemonic structure. The term "other" as a noun can function only in relation to a stated entity. Hence this construct denotes marginality; definition by difference or opposition to what has already been accepted as a standard; identity or existence by default of not being the referent to which the "other" is defined. Otherness, then, denotes dependency or reliance as well as a relationship to that which exists and is defined as self-standing. The reality of otherness can make autonomy, self-definition, and sovereignty nearly impossible.

Throughout human history gender has been but one more basis for marginalization. Yet when considering citizenship and citizenry, the issue of gender is frequently, and pathetically, overlooked. One need merely turn to the groundbreaking document *The Declaration of the Rights of Man and Citizen* (*La Déclaration des Droits de l'Homme et Citoyen*) of 1793, following the French Revolution. Although the document did, in fact, pave the way for the 1948 Universal Declaration of Human Rights—in which "human" refers to all human beings and the "human family"—those who drafted the 1793 document were only thinking of half of the human population.[1] So we would like to address the problematic negotiation between rights (both the exclusion from and fight for rights) based on matters of nation/nationality/nationhood and those linked to gender. When considering exile, are marginality and exclusion gravely compounded if the exiled individual or collective is female?

Femaleness intensifies homelessness and statelessness. Until the early twentieth century throughout the world, women were without a country, a home(land), or a state that granted and protected their rights as individuals—rights that from a twenty-first century, first-world theoretical (not necessarily de facto) perspective are often taken for granted (see, for example, Articles Six and Seven of the *Universal Declaration of Human Rights*, which grant the right to recognition everywhere as a person before the law, and in which everyone is equal before the law and entitled to equal protection of the law without discrimination). Hence femaleness, as it conflates with other de facto marginalizations, must be viewed as an exponential otherness: Other to the nth degree.

Furthermore, those who cross borders—that is, transnational subjects—also often experience a condition marked by painful disorientation, sometimes even ostracism or abjection. Transnationals, hence, form what Homi Bhabha has termed a third space, a hybrid psychic and geographic locus "where the negotiation of incommensurable differences creates a tension peculiar to borderline existence" (218). While entering a new space, a transnational can be accounted for when she belongs to the first or third world; she can also be overlooked and fall between the cracks.

Many factors and events have resulted in the influx of transnational individuals within European nations: World War II and the Holocaust, the existence and collapse or conclusion of fascist dictatorships; the fall of the Wall and the disintegration of the East Bloc; the Balkan conflicts, including the Bosnian Wars; the creation of the European Union; the transience of workers as a result of guest worker programs; economic hardships, revolutions or uprisings in developing nations, to name a few.

Given contemporary global, economic, political, and cultural connections, and the unequal distribution of wealth and resources, migration movements will not disappear. The late twentieth century and the beginning of the twenty-first century have seen fluid borders within Europe that welcome the mobility of citizens of European Union member states, yet these states often close their doors to those from other continents and regions such as Africa and South America, the Near East and the Middle East. Since 1951, the year of the beginning of the creation of the European Union as it exists today, the EU has increasingly been viewed as an economic and political haven for many people from these continents. Furthermore, non-EU nation-states have been attempting for years to gain entrance into the group of the "select few."[2]

Thus in our twentieth and twenty-first centuries, with the opening of borders, we have observed growing groups of transnationals in Europe, many of whom have also come from what is commonly referred to as the second world. France, for example, has seen its highest net migration between 1960 and 2005 at the beginning of this time span. After the 1960s, a lesser yet consistent number of transnationals found their new homes in France in the following decades. Germany has also witnessed a large number of migrants between 1960 and 1965, many of whom are guest workers from Yugoslavia, Spain, and Turkey. Between 1990 and 1995, twice as many migrants could be found in the Federal Republic than ten years later. Spain could hardly account for any transnationals in the period of 1960 to 1985; in 1990, its net migration did not even reach three thousand, yet from 1995 until 2000 we find eight hundred thousand, and from 2000 to 2005 almost three million. A similar pattern can be found in the United Kingdom, though with slightly lower numbers than in Spain. While few transnationals are accounted for from 1960 until the 1990s, in between 1995 and 2000, five hundred thousand lived in the United Kingdom, and even more—one million—in the period from 2000 to 2005.

Many transnational subjects are not exclusively Western, nor are they Eastern, Latin American, African, or European. They are in-between; they are hybrid subjects whose hybridity fosters a sense of otherness and whose, at times, questionable immigration status enshrouds them in a sense of social and legal alienhood. While we, as authors of this text, in no way intend to establish a hierarchy between first-, second-, and third-world exilic or migratory experiences, we use these accepted terms in order to confront the discursive affects. In *Alienhood, Citizenship, Exile, and the Logic of Difference*, Katarzyna Marciniak states that "what is at stake are the emotions generated by the discourse of the category 'alien.'" "Alien," as Marciniak points out, is not a hateful slur, but a legally sanctioned concept in many parts of the world. She argues that only by dissecting discourses that create and sustain alienhood can we "begin to understand the often nuanced impact of discursive violence operating on 'foreign bodies' and its correlation with ethnic and racial violence" (Marciniak xvi). Immigrant bodies are frequently affected by this violence as foreignness connotes inadequacy, strangeness, and even illegitimacy, all engraved by the issue of legal birth.

When gender conflates with alienhood, we must pose the question: how does alien-Woman de-alienate herself? We would propose that Woman's de-alienation is possible through the arduous, complicated, and individualized process of self-definition, of determining who she is, not a reflection of a group, not an incarnation of another's fears or desires, but rather someone she chooses to see herself and to give voice to, someone for all to hear.

In her 1937 epistolary work *Three Guineas* Virginia Woolf affirms, "As a woman, I have no country. As a woman, I want no country. As a woman, my country is the whole world" (129). As becomes evident throughout this book, the common thread that unifies the chapters is the connection between women that liberates them from the constraints of otherness and situates the articulate subject in a psychic place of her own election. Geographic location and the concept of nation and nationality with all that they entail are scrutinized in order to highlight the fact that it is not where one is that fosters belonging and self-identification, but rather one's own conscious subjectivity of who she is that determines and defines her.

We recall Simone de Beauvoir's *The Second Sex*, a book that perfectly delineates gendered otherness: "[H]umanity is male and man defines woman not in herself but as relative to him; she is not regarded as an autonomous being." Sixty years after the publication of her tome, we do not accept de Beauvoir's claim that "man defines woman." Rather we believe that a phallocentric symbolic order (a masculinized dominant discourse) defines woman in relation to the masculine center or standard. Succinctly stated, "To pose Woman is to pose the absolute Other, without reciprocity, denying against all experience that she is a subject, a fellow human being" (Beauvoir 253). Beauvoir asserts,

> Every individual concerned to justify his existence feels that his existence involves an undefined need to transcend himself, to engage in freely chosen projects . . . now, what peculiarly signalizes the situation of woman is that she—a free and autonomous being like all human creatures—nevertheless finds herself living in a world where men [phallocentric symbolic order] compel her to assume the status of the Other . . . The drama of woman lies in this conflict between the fundamental aspirations of every subject (ego)—who always regards the self as the essential—and the compulsions of a situation in which she is the inessential . . . What roads are open to her? How can independence be recovered in a state of dependency? (xxxv)

We also heed Hélène Cixous's scathing denunciation of female otherness and a gendered call to arms that women must insert themselves into their own history by their own actions (196).

Many of the primary works studied within this anthology trace the process of self-definition, the path toward autonomy, the insistence on creating a space where the gendered self simply is, and is not conceived as something by default or in relation to the hegemonic center—be it the ruling class, the mainstream culture, the host country, the dominant discourse, or even a domineering husband or abusive male figure. Although female gender has been a pretext to construct otherness and alienhood by the phallocentric symbolic order (that privileges all that is deemed male or masculine and devalues that which is associated with the feminine), gender becomes a key element in self-definition and identity. As the feminist critic Spike Peterson claims, "Gender refers not to anatomical or biological distinctions but to the social construction, which is always culturally specific, of masculine and feminine as hierarchized and oppositional categories" (41). This definition of gender allows us to underscore the fact that it is precisely because of state-sanctioned inequality (for female citizens, aliens, and exiles) that there are many levels of otherness for the subjects studied here. Only by subverting otherness and vindicating their gender identity do the women (and representations of women) define themselves as autonomous subjects.

The collection partakes in and contributes to what Peterson has deemed "gender-sensitive research." On the one hand, it deconstructs "andro-centric (male-as-norm) accounts," locates "'invisible women," and incorporates "women's experiences and perspectives in the study of humankind," and "on the other, it reconstructs them"—rethinks knowledge, structures, and power relationships in order to create "feminist epistemologies" (48).

When Woman's place—be it individual or collective—continues to be determined by a voice emanating other than from within Her, Woman (as an abstraction and a particular) is conceived of, constructed, and represented as "Other." This is precisely why we underscore the relevance of the primary texts studied and contained within this collection of critical essays. By defining who they are, by voicing their identities, by viewing themselves, these (literary, fictional, cinematic, and historical) women articulate a resounding first-person declaration of self. "I am" is the underlying message.

We thank the our contributors for their time and effort in researching the fate and experiences of women exiles from various cultural, historical, and economic backgrounds. And we extend our gratitude to their patience in waiting to see this book come to fruition. Without them, *Exile Through a Gendered Lens: Women's Displacement in Recent European History, Literature and Film* would not exist in the depth and diversity it does, as indicated by the following chapter summaries.

Chapter Summaries

When Hitler was voted into office in 1933, hundreds of intellectuals fled Germany, struggling to reconcile their creative drive with daily survival, and yearning for the chance to return home. The German playwright Bertolt Brecht was no exception. Neither was his collective, among them a group of women who maintained contact with him throughout their years in exile. In "Exile in Letters: Bertolt Brecht's Collaborators Elisabeth Hauptmann and Margarete Steffin," Paula Hanssen explores the exile experiences of Elisabeth Hauptmann and Margarete Steffin, intellectual and creative women who belonged to Brecht's circle of collaborating writers. With the help of their letters to Brecht and other intellectuals, including the German cultural critic Walter Benjamin, Hanssen shows how these women dealt with their experiences of transience while displaced from their families, careers, and countries. Although their lives differed greatly, both their professional and their personal relationships with Brecht during their years of exile paradoxically underscored their value to Brecht's literary production, yet undermined their creative autonomy.

Mary Thrond studies María Teresa León's narrative works *Memoria de la melancolía* (*Memory of Melancholy*) and *Juego limpio* (*Fair Game*) within the context of present-day democratic Spain. León's writings recover the democratic voices suppressed during Francoism in order to integrate them into history. Thrond focuses on the author's indomitable drive to write, her "enfermedad incurable" (incurable disease). As Thrond states, "Driven by the passion for truth, León wanted to ensure that the Republican voices, which Franco's Fascist regime had censored and erased, be preserved for the Spanish people and for World History." León has poetically preserved history and reconstructed the collective identity of the exiled. Through her polyphonic discourse—alternating between first and third persons—in her memoirs, the author attempts to reconcile her identity and that of her Republican compatriots.

Kimberle López studies the narrative of Argentine exile Alicia Dujovne Ortiz, whose autobiographical novel traces the family tree of the protagonist-narrator Alicia, a journalist from Buenos Aires living in exile in France during Argentina's Dirty War of the late 1970s and early 1980s. When the protagonist's teenage daughter declares that she will leave Paris for the Amazon in search of her roots, Alicia sarcastically retorts that the only roots she will find are those of trees. The daughter of European immigrants, Alicia is currently exiled in Europe, and her only homeland is constructed psychically through remembrance. As López states, "[T]he narrator takes us on a journey from the time of Christopher Columbus through diverse waves of immigration and into the late twentieth century when Alicia opts for exile in France [a kind of "reverse immigration"] over oppression in Argentina." Jewish and Catholic, Russian and Spanish, Argentine yet exiled in France, the protagonist is a trans-Atlantic hybrid whose ancestors were both victims and victimizers, conquistadors and conquered indigenous peoples, Inquisitors and heretics burned by the Inquisition. By uncovering her family tree of generations of eternal immigrants, Alicia discovers her "diasporic identity." The protagonist incarnates the diaspora and symbolizes those who are perpetually strangers in a strange land. Alicia thus represents not only her personal exile but also the history of Argentina as a homeland of immigrants.

In "Writing from the Margins, Writing in the Margins: Christa Wolf's *Medea*," Adelheid Eubanks discusses how one of Germany's most influential writers since 1961 relates the mythological figure Medea to postunification Germany and to Wolf's own situation. For Christa Wolf, Brecht's East German compatriot—both were citizens of the German Democratic Republic, founded in 1949 and dissolved in 1990, shortly after the fall of the Wall—exile was less a geographic displacement than a colonization by the West, an "intellectual exile." In light of the *Literaturstreit* (literature battle) in which West German critics and intellectuals debated the question of whether or not East German writers could still be considered artists when their point of reference, the East German state, no longer existed, Christa Wolf embarked on a voluntary and temporary geographic exile to the United States, where she worked on her first major postreunification novel *Medea*. When Medea was published in 1996 (the English translation appeared in 1998), the literary scene was introduced to a modern(ized) Medea, one who becomes comprehensible as woman, victim, and outsider. In the context of political oppression, especially under the former East German totalitarian regime, Wolf's Medea attained new meaning. And in the context of recent German history as well as the history of Western civilization, it posed many questions concerning "identities" and "identity." According to Eubanks, Wolf speaks with and through Medea when she says, "Ich habe nachempfinden können, wie man sich fühlen muss, wenn man wurzellos ist." (I was able to empathize how one feels when one is rootless.) It is Medea's, Wolf's, and East Germans' rootlessness in general that Eubanks analyzes as the novel's treatment of exile, displacement, and border existence.

Migrant women as they are represented in films by and about women are the topic of Isolina Ballesteros's chapter "Female Transnational Migrations and Diasporas in European 'Immigration Cinema.'" Immigration films made by women give their female subjects a voice that is often at odds with much of the general assumptions on female immigration, and subvert classical conventions of narrative and visual subordination trying to redefine the film aesthetic in order to address the spectator "Other." These films emphasize the essential role of female communities for adaptation and interracial coexistence and reflect on cultural and religious aspects that affect and frequently prevent or delay women's full integration in the adopted country. Ballesteros emphasizes the different way women portray the relationship between the local and the migrant "Other": they are less interested in romanticizing the encounters between the locals and migrants than in exposing the commodification of women's bodies either in the domestic sphere or as a consequence of sexual tourism, and in highlighting the importance of family reunification and the role of women's solidarity in the creation and perpetuation of diasporas. As a way to illustrate the aforementioned aspects, Isolina Ballesteros analyzes the films *Flores de otro mundo/ Flowers from Another World* by Icíar Bollaín (1999); *Inch'Allah dimanche/God Willing, It's Sunday* by Yamina Benguigui (2001); *Extranjeras/Female Foreigners* by Helena Taberna (2002); and *Bhaji on the Beach* (1993) by Gurinder Chadha. Concentrating on women immigrants' interaction with diasporic and adopted communities, these four films ignore widespread yet incomplete media sensationalist discourses on female migration and present alternatives to immigration films that opt for stories about women caught in "no-exit" situations and that are constructed in terms of exploitation, seclusion, and isolation.

Migration is also the topic of Gesa Zinn's chapter "Souls in Transit: Exilic Journeys in Fatih Akin's *The Edge of Heaven* (2007)" in which Zinn describes the various exilic journeys the main characters in *The Edge of Heaven* engage in on their way to self-discovery. Departing from death/pain, their travels take them to new heights inwardly and outwardly. Foreigners to others and to themselves, they live in limbo, outside the mythical circle of life, a state viewers of the films experience as a result of the space and time configurations of Fatih's film text, which invokes in them the notion of *Zerstreuung* (diaspora). Through the characters' criss-crossings and other spatial and temporal markers, according to Zinn, *The Edge of Heaven* heightens the very space of transit and transition. Not atypical for many films, including the genre of the road movie, from which Akin borrows, this film does not emphasize the female traveling experience per se, but does underline women's souls transitioning and arriving at a new "home," something denied the male protagonist, who, as the foreigner, will never arrive.

Applying feminist scholar Demaris Wehr's theory of liberating archetypes that posits that feminist appropriation and rewriting of stagnant patriarchal archetypes can lead to a liberating, feminist symbolic order, Maureen Tobin Stanley discerns liberating myths in Bollaín's filmic text *Te doy mis ojos*. In her chapter, titled "Liberating Mythography: The Intertextual Discourse between Mythological Banishment and Domestic Violence as Exile in *Te doy mis ojos*," Tobin Stanley argues that through the intertextual dialogue between the cinematic central plot and mythological stories, which are artistically presented by the masters of Spain's Golden Age, Bollaín's plot becomes one of liberation. She analyzes a victim's experience of domestic violence as a type of exile in *Te doy mis ojos*. As the battered protagonist Pilar learns to "read" artworks by Rubens, Titian, El Greco, and Velázquez, among others, she begins to understand the underlying power structure and ultimately sees herself within the works. Hence the Golden Age artworks incorporated by Bollaín, as objective correlatives, invite the viewer to draw parallels between the female lead and the artistic texts. The juxtaposition between the ecclesiastical art (Velázquez's *Cardenal de Borja*, Estévez's *El Cardenal de Borbón*, Titian's *Paulo III*, Morales's *La Dolorosa*) and its secular counterparts reflects the tension between the rigid, hierarchical patriarchal structure of the Roman Catholic Church, which prescribes gender norms, and the sensuality and Kristevian *jouissance* depicted in Titian's *Danae recibiendo la lluvia de oro* and Rubens's *Las tres gracias* as well as his *Orfeo y Eurídice*. Baroque art thus becomes a window into two irreconcilable symbolic orders, one of which is the source of the protagonist's "domestic exile." Through the mythological subjects like exiled Eurydice, she learns that home is found through joy, through support, and, most important, within herself.

Our book invites readers to learn about and identify with women's exilic existences and alienhoods. Through the vicarious experience of transience and foreignness, we explore and confront what Julia Kristeva deems "the foreigner within ourselves." It is our hope that a closer look at the "Other" outside and inside of us will bring to light not only differences but also commonalities and, in the process, pave the way for a deeper understanding of the many artificial barriers between us as human beings and individuals in an increasingly more globalized world.

Notes

1. This is explored in detail in Maureen Tobin Stanley's article "Female Voices of Resistance in Neus Català's *De la resistencia y la deportación: The Triumph of Life, Dignity, and Solidarity during the Holocaust*" in *Female Exiles in Twentieth and Twenty-first Century Europe*, edited by Maureen Tobin Stanley and Gesa Zinn (New York: Palgrave Macmillan, 2007).

2. Many have succeeded in joining the founding group of six: Belgium, France, Germany, Italy, Luxembourg, and the Netherlands (Denmark, Ireland, and the U.K. joined in 1973; Greece in 1981; Spain in 1986; Austria, Finland, and Sweden in 1995; Portugal in 1996; and Cyprus, the Czech Republic, Hungary, Malta, Slovakia, and Slovenia in 2004; along with the former Baltic republics Latvia, Estonia, Lithuania,

Bulgaria, and Romania in 2007). Others, like Croatia, the former Yugoslav Republic of Macedonia, and Turkey, are awaiting approval (*Europa* n. pag.).

Works Cited

Beauvoir, Simone de. *The Second Sex*. London: New English Library, 1970 (1st ed. Gallimard 1949). Print.

Bhabha, Homi. *Location of Culture*. London: Routledge, 1994. Print.

Cixous, Hélène. "The Laugh of the Medusa." *New French Feminisms*. Ed. Elaine Marks and Isabelle de Courtivron. New York: Schocken, 1981. 253.

Kristeva, Julia. *Strangers to Ourselves*. Trans. Leon S. Roudiez. New York: Columbia UP, 1991. Print.

Marciniak, Katarzyna. *Alienhood, Citizenship, Exile, and the Logic of Difference*. Minneapolis: Minnesota UP, 2006. Print.

Peterson, V. Spike. "Gendered Nationalism: Reproducing 'Us' versus 'Them.'" *The Women and War Reader*. Ed. Lois Lorentzen and Jennifer Turpin. New York: New York UP, 1998. 41–49. Print.

Wehr, Demaris. *Jung and Feminism—Liberating Archetypes*. London: Routledge, 1988. Print.

Woolf, Virginia. *Three Guineas*. Toronto: Harcourt, 2006 (1st ed. 1938). Print.

1

Exile in Letters

Bertolt Brecht's Collaborators Elisabeth Hauptmann and Margarete Steffin

Paula Hanssen

Overview

Bertolt Brecht and other famous German authors went into exile in 1933 to escape the Hitler regime and World War II. Less well known were the exile experiences of Brecht's collaborators. Two of his coauthors, Elisabeth Hauptmann and Margarete Steffin, maintained correspondence that details their lives in exile on two different continents. Hauptmann had worked on Brecht's plays in Berlin and escaped to the United States while Steffin remained in Europe and helped Brecht write some of his well-known plays, like The Good Person of Sezuan *and* Mother Courage. *Their letters detail their everyday lives as well as their emotional lives. Their paradoxical relationship with Brecht inspired them to write short stories, poetry, and plays, as well as ensured their position in his circle, reducing the possibility of their creative autonomy. This epistolary study presents a biographical and literary itinerary, a journey from a new beginning in exile to frustrated hopes that follow female talent through serpentine paths that lead to their work as coauthors with Brecht.*

For this chapter, I used letters from the Bertolt Brecht Archive (BBA) and the Elisabeth Hauptmann Archive (EHA) in Berlin, as well as from secondary literature about Hauptmann. The Steffin letters and those of her friends were published for the most part in a collection by Stephan Hauck, Margarete Steffin *Briefe an berühmte Männer*, and also in Hartmut Reiber's *Grüss den Brecht* and other primary and secondary literature listed.

This chapter is a biographical window into the lives of two women, Margarete Steffin (b. 1908 Berlin–d. 1941 Moscow) and Elisabeth Hauptmann (1897 Peckelsheim-Westphalia–1973 Berlin), who left Germany in 1933 and were for the most part marginalized and overshadowed for various reasons: the limbo of exile and—for Steffin—the limbo of serious illness, their secondary status as women within their society, their self-relegation to auxiliary roles within Bertolt Brecht's literary entourage, and their position as two among several other literary collaborators who consistently shared Brecht's attention on collaborative writing efforts but not his fame or success.

I began to research these women in graduate school through secondary literature but found little on specific contributions. Brecht's translator, John Willet, wrote that Hauptmann chose "to sink herself in the collective and merger her literary identity with his" (Willett 133). Discouraged by the director of the Brecht Archive in 1989, who claimed that no Hauptmann manuscripts were there, I heard from Brecht's son Stefan Brecht that there were texts, and that there was a collection of copies at the Houghton Library at Harvard. In 1990 in Berlin, I was able to finally read the materials that had never been catalogued in the Elisabeth Hauptmann Archive and start the process of finding some clues to her contributions to specific texts. For Margarete Steffin there were reliable biographies and texts, and the excellent collection of letters by Stefan Hauck.

The study that follows does not aim to portray Steffin and Hauptmann as icons of feminism who triumphed personally and professionally. These two exceptionally talented literary women were instrumental and essential to Bertolt Brecht's literary, filmic, and theatrical productions that revolutionized how scholars and the populace regarded theater. And yet they had been relegated to footnotes and musty archives until the publication of recent biographies and compilations of correspondence. Books include Inge Gellert's *Margarete Steffin: Konfutze versteht nichts von Frauen: Nachgelassene Texte* (*Margarete Steffin: Confucius Doesn't Understand Anything about Women*), Sabine Kebir's *Ich fragte nicht nach meinem Anteil: Elisabeth Hauptmanns Arbeit mit Bertolt Brecht* (*I Did Not Ask about My Share: Elisabeth Hauptmann's Work with Bertolt Brecht*), this author's volume *Elisabeth Hauptmann: Brecht's Silent Collaborator*, Stefan Hauck's *Margarete Steffin Briefe an berühmte Manner: Walter Benjamin, Bertolt Brecht, Arnold Zweig* (*Margarete Steffin: Letters to*

Famous Men: Walter Benjamin, Bertolt Brecht, Arnold Zweig), and Hartmut Reiber's *Grüß den Brecht: Das Leben von Margarete Steffin* (*Greet Brecht: The Life of Margarete Steffin*).

As noteworthy as these studies are, they have not clearly shed light on the gendered experience in exile of these two writers. Their paradoxical relationship with Brecht, on the one hand, inspired them to write short stories, poetry, and plays, as well as ensured their position—although often in secretarial functions—in the literary circle, while on the other hand, reduced the possibility of creative autonomy. Their letters express their ideas, their desires, and their context. The letter as form is a vehicle for that self-expression because of the letter's multivalency; according to Janet Altman, it is "a linguistic phenomenon, a real-life form, and an instrument of amorous or philosophical communication" (5). Steffin's and Hauptmann's letters were that, but they can also be read as literature that maintained their connection with friends and colleagues, and described many places they experienced in exile. Whether in a hospital or clinic in Denmark or Switzerland or Moscow, Steffin describes her experiences connecting with the people around her and with Brecht in sonnets and stories. Hauptmann portrays the United States and its capitalist system, then her fear of isolation, of poverty, of never finding meaningful work and relationships.

The epistolary form is an intermediary: the author can choose to emphasize the connection, or the distance between author and recipient. Both Steffin and Hauptmann wrote to bridge the separation by describing it; they portray their desire for more emotional connection to fill the void, and describe their experiences and reactions to their context (Altman 13). Their letters often include the stress of continuing their work and at the same time working for others; their health concerns, especially Steffin, who suffered from tuberculosis; and their search for publication venues and income. Independent women of their times, they were driven to explore their idea of autonomy as writers, and enjoyed collaboration on texts with Brecht and friends. Their letters are their testament to their struggles as women and writers in exile.

Hence it is my hope to spur on the study of these two women writers who were unable to maintain independence. Perhaps by shedding light on Steffin's and Hauptman's lives as exiles frustrated by the lack of publishing venues, as writers whose circumstances impeded them from honing their craft, scholars and readers alike will be driven to explore the fruits of Steffin's and Hauptmann's intellectual labors and discover their value as writers in their own right, not simply as Brecht's scribes. My epistolary study presents a biographical and literary itinerary, a journey from a new beginning in exile to frustrated hopes that follow female talent through serpentine paths that lead to their major life work as coauthors with Brecht. These women are a testament to the reality that liberalism and socially progressive thought regarding class did not necessarily afford the same to matters of gender, and in essence relegated women to auxiliary—that is, noncentral, nonautonomous—roles.

Elisabeth Hauptmann

Elisabeth Flora Charlotte Hauptmann was born June 20, 1897, in Northrhein-Westphalia as the daughter of the physician and privy to the court, Dr. Clemens Hauptmann, and his German-American wife, Josephine Diestelhorst. The children were taught at home, had music and language lessons, and performed their own plays. In 1918, Hauptmann became a teacher, a career deemed suitable for women of her class, and taught in Germany's rural eastern provinces with their wealthy military families. However, she loathed the hierarchical power structure and politics of the wealthy and conservative Junker society, which dominated all the higher civil offices and the officer corps in Prussia.

In 1922, Hauptmann moved to Berlin, worked as a secretary, wrote, immersed herself in Berlin's culture during the liberal era of the Weimar Republic, and even joined the German Communist Party. She met Brecht in 1924 at a friend's party; he was so impressed that she took notes of their conversation that he asked his publisher to hire her for his latest collection of poetry, *Hauspostille* (*Breviary for the Home*). She incorporated two of her own poems, "O Moon of Alabama" and the "Benares Song," into Brecht's *Breviary for the Home*, without a credit for her work. This inauspicious beginning is only the first example of Hauptmann's contributions to Brecht's works, which became ever more substantial; those two poems of hers in *Breviary*, for example, were then later used in their opera *Aufstieg und Fall der Stadt Mahagonny* (*The Rise and Fall of the City Mahagonny*).

Until 1933, Hauptmann wrote and published her own stories and did research for—as well as contributed to—practically all of Brecht's works. She published the short story "Julia without Romeo" in the magazine *Das Leben* in 1926; and her story "Bessie So and So," about a Salvation Army officer who saves her troop in the San Francisco earthquake of 1906, appeared in 1928 in *Uhu*, a popular monthly magazine that featured the new, emancipated woman of the Weimar Republic, Hauptmann's milieu. Brecht had already dedicated the first version of their 1925 play *Mann ist Mann* (*A Man is a Man*) to Hauptmann, and wrote that the only part of the production he did himself was the binding (*Berliner und Frankfurter Ausgabe*2, 408).[1]

Her translation of John Gay's *The Beggar's Opera* in 1927 inspired their work together with Kurt Weill on the biggest German box office hit of 1928, *Die Dreigroschenoper* (*The Threepenny Opera*). Brecht, then, in 1929, suggested that they work on *Happy End*, a musical, with the composer Kurt Weill, based on her research on the Salvation Army, which she wrote under the pseudonym Dorothy Lane. Their close working relationship was a very personal as well as professional one, though the work was always paramount. Brecht's marriage in 1929 to Helene Weigel, the actress and mother of two of his children, did not change their collaborative efforts; Hauptmann maintained the collaboration with Brecht on a professional level. In 1931, she married the editor Kurt Hacke, only to divorce him in 1932.

Hauptmann contributed much to Brecht's works with her translations, mostly from texts in English. She found Arthur Waley's translations of Japanese and Chinese texts, and translated his version of the Japanese Nô-play *Taniko* (*Taniko oder der Wurf ins Tal*) (Taniko or the Casting into the Valley), which she also published in the theater journal *Der Scheinwerfer* ("The Lights") in 1929. *Der Ja-Sager* (*The Yes-Sayer*) and *Die Maßnahme* (*The Measures Taken*) are based on the Waley text and on the same theme of the needs of the individual versus the group. Their last Berlin collaboration went back to Hauptmann's adaptation of and translation from Shakespeare's *Measure for Measure* in 1932 with Ludwig Berger, the director of the Berlin *Volksbühne* (people's stage), which became *Die Rundköpfe und die Spitzköpfe* (*The Roundheads and the Peakheads*). The rise of fascism squelched that creative freedom. Germany's Fascist political upheaval and the burning of the *Reichstag* in February

1933 prompted Brecht and his family to flee, first to France. In spite of the danger for Communists and intellectuals, Hauptmann remained in Berlin and arranged for the safe transport of most of their papers. Her letters describe her dilemma trying to save her and Brecht's manuscripts from confiscation, and her decision to immigrate to St. Louis, where her sister would support her for the "few months" of Hitler's popularity in Europe. That decision was made partly because of her strained relationship with Brecht, who apparently had criticized her efforts in Berlin to save the manuscripts; she explained her decision to their friend Walter Benjamin: "[My sister] is taking care of everything, ticket, consulate etcetera for me . . . I decided to take this invitation at a time when I was discouraged and depressed about the behavior of some people for whom I had stuck my neck out . . . I don't know if it's right, and in any case it doesn't need to be for more than four months" (Elizabeth Hauptmann Archive 11/15–20).[2]

In late 1933, the Gestapo searched her room and then arrested her for interrogation. As soon as she obtained her release, she left for Paris, where Brecht, Margarete Steffin, and many other German intellectuals waited, naively hoping to return to Germany. In Paris, Hauptmann planned to travel to the United States by ship, and decided to break off her relationship with Brecht, using the letter as an intermediary to emphasize their past and then a future independence: "Let's stop this kind of relationship, Brecht. You seem to be happy . . . And I, believe me, will find what I want, a great and tender relationship with another person in this work, with a *complete* break from you. Our relationship was somewhat clumsy and rough, but it was the best working friendship you've ever had and I will have. Your Bess Hauptmann" (BBA 430/133–34).[3] Her resolve for a complete break seems to have faded with her sense of isolation in the United States. After the first weeks of euphoria in St. Louis in January 1934, Hauptmann became depressed by the isolation from her work with Brecht. Many of her manuscripts, which had been sent along with Brecht's to Denmark, were missing. On February 26, 1934, she wrote Brecht: "Now I'm beginning to despair because so much is missing. Have you found the 'Polly scene' and the 'Ballad of World Approval'?" (BBA 480/104).[4]

Although the letters often describe life in the States in positive terms, even the promising contacts with influential individuals and publishing possibilities, her letters to Benjamin contain reflections about the United States and Europe, often with lyrical passages and beautiful metaphors about her struggles to find work and connections. Looking for work in New York City had been unsuccessful for the most part. The publishing industry was impenetrable, like a thick wall, and her attempt to fit in, to belong, is expressed as her desire to find a hole in that sturdy wall. She wrote to Benjamin on May 8, 1934: "Another attempt to find a hole (not just in a fence, but in a sturdy wall), through which I could slip. The walls are so well built and well cemented that there's no hole to find. Everyone advises me to sit down and write a novel, but that one has to sleep and to eat in the meantime doesn't interest anyone (probably for good reason)" (EHA 89).[5] The imagery perfectly metaphorizes the exiled author's lack of engagement and her loneliness. This fits with what the scholar Roberta Rubenstein, in her research, termed "a longing for belonging." Hauptmann is separated from a sense of belonging by a complex, multifaceted barrier; her exclusion is the result of her creative and professional impotence, geographic displacement, cultural difference, ideological clashes, and the disadvantage of gender.

Hauptmann's publishing projects went mostly unrealized, such as a volume she planned for young readers about women like the union organizer Molly Maguire and the socialist organizer Rosa Luxemburg (EHA 348). Autobiographical stories in letters were not published until later in her collected works, *Julia ohne Romeo* (*Julia without Romeo*), titled after the first short story in the book. Another story is titled "*Im Greyhound Unterwegs*" (In a Greyhound). The summer heat in St. Louis sets up Hauptmann's story about traveling on a Greyhound bus to New York City and back. She describes the bus driver's derogatory remarks about the "blacks" in the back of the bus, the segregated rest stop, and then her respect for the black women who endured the discrimination with dignity. Hauptmann's ideological clash with her host environment is evident in her disdain for racism, and also in her Marxist critique of the arts as a vehicle for capitalism. She writes, "Broadcasting is a strange thing here— industry finances art and the artists—the grand Saturday afternoon performances of the Metropolitan Operas (which cost a fortune) are, for example, sponsored by the 'Lucky Strike' cigarette factory. In the intermissions and afterwards the text is explained or the main singers are interviewed. Music-loving smokers smoke 'Lucky Strike' to support the company and make the broadcasts possible . . . It's really interesting and this relationship between art and business has never bothered me so little" (BBA 480/101–2).[6]

Despite his work with another talented collaborator now in exile, Margarete Steffin, Brecht still wanted Hauptmann's opinion on his work and he sent texts for her comments, such as the play they had begun in Berlin, *The Roundheads and the Peakheads*. Hauptmann's handwriting is on the original typescripts, and she described her work in a letter to Brecht, hoping for royalties in the event that it would be performed (hardly likely in Denmark). Hauptmann also claimed credit for the idea for the play, which she got from Kleist's novella *Michael Kohlhaas*, and asked for royalties similar to those assigned for *The Threepenny Opera*: "I'd like to be included at the *Threepenny* rate . . . You can count it as collaboration or work as distribution consultant" (BBA 480/94).[7] She had not found an American publisher, despite letters of introduction from Vicki Baum, author of the popular novel *Grand Hotel*, and from Lion Feuchtwanger, a writer and colleague of Brecht's. Hauptmann had no U.S. publications, and very few to show from Germany, most of which appear under a pseudonym. She was able to publish one story, titled *Gastfeindschaft (Inhospitality)*, in an anthology for exiles, *Dreißig neue Erzaehler des neuen Deutschlands (Thirty New Authors of the New Germany)*, about an unemployed man grudgingly invited to be the guest of a wealthy German family on Christmas Eve. This creative and literary reality perfectly communicates Hauptmann's own situation and exile in the United States. Because of the barriers to cultural, ideological, gender, and literary belonging, Hauptmann—a guest in a host environment—is, like her protagonist, an object of "inhospitality." She does not feel that she is welcome, and, moreover, she does not have a place in which she feels at home. Such disappointment was the theme in a greeting for Brecht in December 1934: "Best Wishes for 1935, fondly, your Bess. Please write, one is so alone here."[8] The alienation seemed insurmountable and she saw no end in sight. In January she wrote, "It has been exactly a year since I arrived and it seems like eternity. Write to me. I want to know how long I'll have to be here" (BBA 480/22).[9]

The autobiographical nature of letters offers evidence, as John Paul Eakin suggests in *How Our Lives Become Stories*, about how individuals experience their sense of being "I" (4). For example, Hauptmann's isolation from writing brought on depression; she felt so isolated that she even questioned her own memories of her intense collaborative work with Brecht in this letter to Walter Benjamin from St. Louis in 1935:

> Oh God, it has been months, almost years between now and the time that I saw you all last. I know that if my ship doesn't get to Europe soon through some happy coincidence that it won't happen; anxiety already affects my sight and sometimes, when I'm forced . . . to mention the name Brecht it seems a lie that I spent up to 18 hours a day for years with him, and I can't express those memories because I don't want to misrepresent anything. Someone asked about *The Measures Taken* and suddenly I remembered a strange apartment in Augsburg where we transposed the Japanese "No" play and sent the first scenes to Ihering [Berlin critic] in Berlin for printing.[10]

Clearly, Hauptmann had previously defined herself in relation to Brecht and the literary circle. Without them, she doubts not only herself but also her ability to recollect. Memory is often selective and reflects the subjective perception of what was; yet Hauptmann does not rely on her subjective account of the past. Not only was she unable to have economic and creative autonomy in exile, she was incapable of defining herself as an individual writer, separate from her previous network of collaboration.

For Hauptmann, identity in interconnectedness began to reemerge with her position as a teacher when she was issued a "quota visa" and worked as a German instructor, treating the students like an interdependent group. In May 1935 she wrote, "For me teaching at the college is still very interesting. I have a group that would go through thick and thin with me" (BBA 480/11).[11] The job was funded through FERA, the Federal Emergency Relief Administration in the Roosevelt years: "I earn—because it's a 'FERA' position to create jobs—$45/month. Of that I have to spend at least $5 for transportation. And I'm not allowed to wear mended hosiery and my hair has to be done. I'm not allowed to look tired, have to be well dressed and the grammar hour has to be interesting, like entertainment" (EHA 354).[12] Although employed, Hauptmann could not

become self-sufficient. As she stated, the nominal payment was rein-
vested in arriving at and dressing for the position.

In 1935, Brecht and the composer Hanns Eisler had been invited
to help with a production of Brecht's play *The Mother* in New York
City. In October Brecht sent a telegram from the ship to New York,
asking if Hauptmann would meet him and help to coordinate living
space. She went, conveniently furloughed from the teaching position
in St. Louis while the school was closed for renovation, arranged
for an apartment, and accompanied Brecht and Eisler to rehearsals, especially to help them communicate in English. Both Brecht
and Eisler were apparently unhappy with the production and tried
to interrupt the rehearsals, which finally resulted in their ejection
from the theater. The play only ran a few days, but Brecht remained
in New York working on projects with Hauptmann for a few weeks
until early February. He wrote her in St. Louis on February 6, 1936,
suggesting they work together in Europe soon: "Dear Bess, I'm leaving. And hope you come soon. It was really good that you guided me
in the USA—as it was always planned. I thank you, dear Bess. And I
won't forget anything. I won't leave you in St. Louis, . . . As soon as
I'm in Denmark, I'll force the issue" (BFA 28/544).[13] The promised
help with a move to Europe or to the Soviet Union never material-
ized. This incident and subsequent correspondence proves revealing
of the continued dynamic between Brecht and Hauptmann. Brecht
had no qualms about placing demands on Hauptmann—to travel
950 miles from St. Louis to New York, to make accommodations for
him, to serve as his interpreter—, which she fulfilled. The promise
of support was not realistic in light of his situation as an unemployed Marxist refugee from Fascism—although a Marxist, Brecht
was justifiably wary of the system in the Soviet Union—and someone responsible for a family, as well as for his young collaborator
Margarete Steffin.

Although she kept busy in St. Louis from 1936 to 1940, working again as a teacher, Hauptmann continued to support Brecht's
literary enterprises, writing and reviewing his and Steffin's manuscripts, while hoping to move on to New York City. In June 1939,
Hauptmann thanked Brecht for sending his new work, the *Galileo*
text, and offered to comment on it (BBA 1396/79). By December
1939, she was gaining some independence teaching German at a
Christian Science College and studying French. She also wrote for

the *Young Worker Newspaper* in Prague, and for a broadcast called "Labor against Nazism."

By 1939, the Brecht circle in Denmark included his family and two collaborators, Margarete Steffin and a Danish actress and journalist, Ruth Berlau. With the growing Fascist presence in Denmark, they moved to Sweden and planned to go on to the United States. Southern California was home to many German and Austrian intellectuals, like the writer Lion Feuchtwanger, the director Berthold Viertel and his wife, and the actor Peter Lorre. Though she knew Brecht would settle in California, Hauptmann moved on to the New York City area.

In New York, Hauptmann met and collaborated with another exile, Horst Baerensprung, former social democrat and head of the Magdeburg police, who had immigrated to China when Hitler came to power and taught criminal justice at Shanghai University, then later at Harvard (Kebir 186). Baerensprung, who shared her interests in politics and in Asia, became the partner with whom Hauptmann felt comfortable. She wrote weekly broadcasts in German for CBS shortwave, read for broadcast by Baerensprung, and also wrote his memoirs (EHA 146, 148, 149). This work with Baerensprung supported Hauptmann's concept of self as writer, seen in a description of their working relationship that she had written for Baerensprung's daughter in 1954. Baerensprung loved to tell stories but was inept at writing, so that, as Hauptmann claims, she was the actual author of the memoir and of the radio broadcasts—similar to her work with Brecht (EHA 181). She writes, "I provided well-rehearsed questions, for which I had read untold numbers of books and I consulted other friends who had been in China . . . [T]he memoir is therefore mine, my intellectual property, even the radio broadcasts we wrote so that he could speak every week on the radio. There too he could not be persuaded to write a line himself or to use dictation" (EHA 462).[14]

Although Hauptmann was gainfully employed as a writer, yet again she was cast in the shadow of a male presence and public personality. She was productive and felt useful but, sadly, received little authorial credit.

Ruth Berlau, who had moved to New York City, became the catalyst for Hauptmann's return to collaboration with Brecht. Berlau was working for the Office of War Information in New York City in the early 1940s, broadcasting in Danish to Denmark, when she asked Hauptmann to help Brecht for two hours weekly. Hauptmann initially baulked, "Two hours for Brecht? Whoever works for Brecht works no less than 24 hours a day!" (qtd. in Berlau 9).[15] However, when Berlau was admitted to a psychiatric hospital with extreme depression and suffering from alcoholism, Hauptmann was drawn into the Brecht circle again. She visited Berlau and then wrote to Brecht on January 9, 1945, about bringing Ruth some clothing, as long as Baerensprung did not learn of it (BBA 211/23). Besides helping Brecht maintain contact with Berlau, Hauptmann ran the office, recorded minutes, and maintained a budget (BBA, Cohen Collection). Again, Hauptmann subordinated her talent and usefulness to an auxiliary function as secretary for the think tank Council for a Democratic Germany, which included intellectuals such as the chair and theologian Paul Tillich from Union Seminary and Columbia University, Horst Baerensprung, the director Berthold Viertel, and the American theologian Reinhold Niebuhr.

Brecht appointed her editor for the English versions of his plays in his *Collected Works*, translated by Eric Bentley. Brecht had given Hauptmann *plein pouvoir* (full power) to check Bentley's translations, causing Bentley some consternation as to his role as mediator for the American public. Bentley wrote that Hauptmann even added whole passages to the translation, and when Bentley asked if they were appropriate Brecht would say, "yes, yes, leave it in" (qtd. in Bentley 25). At first blush, the *plein pouvoir* afforded to Hauptmann by Brecht affirms Hauptmann's talent, knowledge, and expertise. Upon closer scrutiny, though, her role is cemented as secondary, never central. Bentley's mistrust of Hauptmann, who happened to be a woman, was only allayed by a word from the (gendered) authority, Brecht himself.

When Baerensprung decided to return to his family in Braunschweig, Germany, in 1946, Hauptmann accepted Brecht's invitation to move to California. Brecht wrote, "I'm so glad that she'll work with me again for the first time; she is irreplaceable" (*Briefe* 524).[16] She and Brecht worked on several collaborative projects, such as the 1947 film story *The Coat, a Film by Bertolt Brecht and Elisabeth Hauptmann from the Novella by Gogol* (EHA 41). The collaboration was short lived; after Brecht appeared for an interview before the House Committee on Unamerican Activities in 1947, he flew on to Switzerland with Weigel, intending to move on to Berlin and wait for Hauptmann and composer Paul Dessau. Dessau married Hauptmann in 1948, but soon flew on to Europe, leaving her to wrap up loose ends and raise money to pay for her ticket back to Germany.

Hauptmann's last letters from the United States describe her frustrations with her dire financial state. It was clear she was looking for independence; she rejected the "just a woman" status. She described her plight with irony and an attempt at humor: "It is hard not to be impatient. To try to make it when one is older, alone, i.e. without connections, without a couple of influential friends, is hard . . . There are only three ways for a woman: either she makes herself irreplaceable sexually, or she makes herself irreplaceable in her work, or she blackmails someone when those first two aren't enough. Then there's the other, which classifies her as more than just as a woman: she makes herself completely independent and finds her own influential platform" (BBA, Cohen Collection).[17]

Brecht wrote from Switzerland in September 1948 that Dessau had arrived, and he urged her to come despite health concerns, assuming that Hauptmann, as an American citizen, would have no trouble getting papers for the American zone in Germany. "I'm counting on you, and that we can come to an agreement and start working together. Don't talk yourself into ill health; it's only a question of work. You've been chosen to live to 90 and you'll be complaining enough until then . . . [Hans] Albers wants to take *The Threepenny Opera* on tour; that's also money [in royalties] for you. So get packing" (*Briefe 2*, 467).[18]

But neither Brecht nor Dessau was able to wait for her collaboration and support in what had become the Soviet sector of Berlin and where Brecht and Weigel now directed their own theater company, the Berlin Ensemble. By the time she arrived in February 1949, Brecht had other collaborators, Dessau had begun a relationship with an actress, and Hauptmann was again left on her own to find lodging and connections. Despite the difficult beginning, she was able to carve out a niche in the German Democratic Republic as a *Dramaturg* at the *Berliner Ensemble*, and as the editor of Brecht's *Collected Works* published in East as well as West Germany. She worked with the *Berliner Ensemble* until her death on June 20, 1973.

In regard to the three options Hauptmann viewed as available to women (being irreplaceable sexually, being irreplaceable at work, blackmail when the former two fail), we must consider that all three evince an uneven power structure. The first two service/serve others (one can assume men) and the last corruptly takes the upper hand. Of the three options Hauptmann saw for herself, she chose the least demeaning. She was, without a doubt, essential to Brecht's creative production, yet by making herself "irreplaceable" in his endeavors, she sacrificed her own creative autonomy.

Margarete Steffin

Margarete Steffin's struggle for creative autonomy was in many ways parallel to that of Hauptmann. The contemporary German intellectual community discovered Steffin in a documentary film about her and Brecht in exile by Danish journalist Rudy Hassing: *Unter dem Strohdach: Brecht in Dänemark* (*Under the Straw Roof: Brecht in Denmark*) and then in Inge Gellert's collection of Steffin's works, *Konfutse versteht nichts von Frauen* (*Confucius Doesn't Understand Women*).

She had begun writing plays, short stories, and poems while in school and wrote with such clarity and imagination that she received a literary prize for a school essay. Despite her teachers' efforts to help her obtain a scholarship for high school, her father refused to allow her to attend, as it would separate her from the working class. Determined to educate herself, Steffin read constantly and attended evening lectures at the Berlin Marxist Workers' School (MASCH). She also took private lessons in Russian and enjoyed performing in reciting choruses (*Sprechchöre*). Those interests practically predestined that she would meet Brecht's wife, the actress Helene Weigel, who was very active in Berlin theater programs for the proletariat. Steffin supported herself with clerical work, and in 1926 became a member of a workers' ensemble that depicted workers' lives and the class struggle. She was diagnosed with tuberculosis, which required treatments and surgery for the rest of her short life.

As a student of Helene Weigel, she became one of the main speakers for the *Red Review*, with other famous German actors and dancers in Berlin like Ernst Busch, Valeska Gert, and Lotte Lenya. She got to know Brecht in discussions about his plays as a member of *Gruppe junger Schauspieler* (Young Actors Group); he chose her to play the maid in *Die Mutter* (*The Mother*). After the production Brecht contacted specialists in tuberculosis at the main hospital in Berlin, the *Charité*, who operated on Steffin in February 1932. Their relationship quickly became very personal as well as professional, and she accompanied Brecht to Moscow for the premiere of his film about a proletariat tent camp for the homeless, *Kuhle Wampe*, and went for more treatment in the Crimea.

Steffin's letters to Brecht begin during the sanatorium stay. The routine in the sanatorium was strict, leaving little time for letters or for her own writing: "I feel guilty . . . Even though I haven't been lazy. But half the day is 'lost' with treatment, meals, the afternoon nap of two hours etcetera . . . I speak with the Russian comrades, I try to listen to their views on working women, the church and child labor" (Hauck 51).[19] Her letters, written in a type of pseudojournalistic style, are reminiscent of short newspapers describing the social movements of the day. Her natural curiosity and openness with others, as well as her gift with languages, helped her quickly make connections and to create a sense of community. The idea of the new society under communism intrigued her, and she wrote about interviewing Soviet patients for their views.

Back in Germany with Brecht in June 1932, she felt well enough to begin work as a consistent collaborator, editor, translator, and critic. They began work on the play that Brecht and Hauptmann had started before they left Berlin, *The Roundheads and the Peakheads*. During a hospitalization from November to January 1933 she sent Brecht sonnets like "Today I dreamed that I lay by you" (Hauck 58),[20] as well as a second sonnet about a dream that Brecht had left her, one that suggested the actual end of their lives together. The final verse reads, "I couldn't scream, because I was running / And you were leaving. The brake light shone / Now there's nothing more, I thought. And was silent" (Hauck 58).[21] Clearly this dream encapsulates Steffin's attachment to Brecht and a fear of her silence if separated from him. The silent oneiric "protagonist" reveals the anxiety about an authorial female voice.

After her release from the hospital, Steffin became even more active in the anti-Nazi movement, participating in *Agitprop*, performances of short plays and choral presentations to inspire opposition and criticize the government. It was not long before police arrested the members of *Agitprop* for expressing "Contempt of the Government" in February 1933. She feared another arrest and left Germany for treatment in Switzerland at a German clinic in Agra by Davos. There she was surrounded by Germans who at least tacitly supported the Hitler regime; in response she wrote an article about her treatment in the Soviet Union for the clinic newsletter. She left Agra on June 1 and, instead of returning to Berlin, met Brecht in Paris. From her letter written in May 1933 from the Agra clinic, it had become clear to her that she was not the only "other woman" in Brecht's life. She used Brecht's own allegory about dishonesty, the story of soldiers who were intimate friends, sharing everything, until one discovered the other had lied about having cigarettes. Disappointed, she strove to be honest about her needs and flexible enough not to lose that intimacy and relationship, one that seemed even more important in exile as a source for a sense of belonging: "It's so hard to know you, although (and I think it's the most desirable attribute) it should be easy especially with you . . . (including all friends that I know) everyone assumes that they know you (or want to know you) or not: still everyone expects 'a cigarette' from you. I don't want that. That shouldn't be. But I would like to think—maybe it's not really so?" (Hauck 61).[22]

The cigarette metaphor proves quite revealing. Not only is this form of tobacco a phallic symbol, but it also speaks to a sense of shared intimacy that once consumed is discarded. As one of Brecht's several "other women," Steffin's relationship with him revealed pleasure, use, and consumption.

In Paris she planned to achieve some self-determination and a way to maintain the relationship with Brecht by founding a literary agency for German exiles, the *Deutscher Autoren Dienst* (or DAD, German Authors Agency). Steffin built a clientele of writers and journalists like Egon Kisch, Oskar Maria Graf, and Heinrich and Thomas Mann. Their response was often slow; in one letter to Brecht, who had moved to Denmark, she says that the articles she had received were old and no longer appropriate for publication (Hauck 70). At the end of July 1933 she wrote, "I think it's not good to wait [for direction] until you come here [for the DAD], that will certainly be too late? And by then one should have begun . . . it's unfortunate that the people we had for our agency will slowly start to look for other agencies" (Hauck 84).[23]

Besides her work for the agency she took on editing for others, including Brecht's manuscript *The Threepenny Novel*, Hanns Eisler's song collection *Lieder Gedichte Chöre* (*Songs Poems Choruses*), and

Walter Benjamin's letters from famous Germans, *Deutsche Menschen* (*German People*). She was still consumed by jealousy and the emotional energy she needed to overcome her frustration. She wrote this sonnet of revenge in July of 1933: "Imagine: all the women / you have had come to your bed" (Hauck 65). The tables are turned for Brecht in this dream: women dominate in the poem and demand his services, and in the last line the poetic voice, too, lines up with the women. In her disappointment she wrote, "[T]hen I hear what Helli said to me in Berlin; 'I feel sorry for you, my child' and then I feel sorry for myself" (BBA 654/45).[24] Clearly, Steffin's desire for Brecht is at odds with her wish for professional independence instead of a sentimental-sexual bond and leads to depression or even self-loathing. Her professional dependence on him obfuscates the personal rapport.

Maintaining her Paris apartment for the literary agency became too expensive, so with the help of Brecht and his Danish collaborator, Ruth Berlau, Steffin went to Copenhagen. Brecht had arranged for a doctor for her, brought some of his manuscripts for editing, and discouraged her from writing her own detective novel in mid-February 1934 (Hauck 112). This incident proves quite revealing. Brecht's concern for Steffin's health could be deemed purely altruistic, yet that notion is thrown into question upon his insistence that she devote herself to his manuscripts and set aside her own project. It was soon clear to her that Berlau, too, was Brecht's lover; again she expressed flexibility by letting Brecht know her disappointment— and her emotional dependence: "This will be the last about 'the [jealousy] complex.' Besides some difficult circumstances, I've kept good memories of . . . [the days in Copenhagen] when you were extremely nice and generous with me. That you could be so kind could make me your debtor—but I'm already enslaved" (Hauck 115).[25] The latter adjective and metaphor clearly communicates the relationship of power. Not only is his wish her command, but her will is subordinate to and, in fact, supplanted by his. This metaphor counters the possibility of self-definition and autonomy—be they personal or professional.

Steffin often traveled on a search for opportunities for publication, or work with Brecht away from Denmark, or treatments for the ever-worsening tuberculosis. In 1934, she was in Copenhagen, then

by the end of February in Svendborg, with a few days in Copenhagen for a physical examination to check on the progress of the
tuberculosis. In September of 1934 she traveled to Moscow, and
then to Georgia for treatment from October to January 1935. There
she started her children's play *Wenn er einen Engel hätte* (*If He Only
Had an Angel*). In 1935, she met Brecht in Leningrad and went to
Moscow where they lived together until the end of May. She moved
on to Copenhagen, and in July she lived in Thüro with a friend of
Helene Weigel, the Danish writer Karin Michaelis who had helped
Weigel find housing. In October, she was in Copenhagen while
Brecht was working with Hauptmann and the theater in New York,
until she sailed to Leningrad on December 21. In 1936, she traveled
in Russia, Georgia, and England. In Russia she hoped for a visit from
Brecht, which he declined; she admonished him in a letter: "Even
though I understand that you want to be 'home' for a while, it really
bothers me that I have no 'home.' Nowhere, I always have to find a
space for me and my suitcase, and I can't even buy books, because
where would I keep them? Of course I see that clearly—it's difficult,
even if you write pages about why this is the case, it's still so terrible
that I can't describe it (Hauck 194)."[26]

Steffin's imagery of the "space for me and my suitcase" is parallel
to Hauptmann's "hole . . . in the thick wall." Both elucidate the need
to belong, to create a psychic space called home. Whether it is intimate, geographic, or professional, these two exiled female writers
avidly and actively sought out a niche, yet inevitably always seemed
to rely on Brecht to define their place.

Steffin's ability in Russian helped Brecht with Russian intellectuals, and helped her make connections and even publish. In Moscow
she lived with her friends Michail Kolzow, coeditor for the newspaper *Pravda* and the magazine *Ogonjok*, and his German partner
Maria Osten (Hauck 345) who helped her publish a story in Russian
in *Ogonjok* for 250 rubles.

After the stay in Russia, she traveled on to London to stay with
Brecht in June and July while he looked for work in the film industry before they returned to Denmark. The constant intellectual
stimulation and work did not save her from depression, likely
caused by the isolation, dependence on Brecht, worsening tuberculosis, and lack of permanent housing. These thoughts are almost

an exact parallel to Hauptmann's insecurity and depression that left her sometimes confused about the enormity of the role she played in Brecht's work and about her own talent. Steffin wrote in Danish in 1940 to a friend, "I really want to be productive, but I have to admit to you: always, when I begin writing, I'm anxious that someone will say that I didn't write it myself. And then I stop, or I think that it's not worth anything" (Hauck 36).[27] The collaboration and contribution to Brecht's enterprises stifled Steffin's own creative voice to the point that, as previously indicated, she could no longer take ownership of her own literary conceptions.

By translating novellas, short stories, essays, even novels and dramas from English, Norwegian, Swedish, and Finnish, whether in or out of the hospital, she was able to earn a meager living. Her drive to write, even when she was supposed to be relaxing and recuperating, was paramount. She wrote to Walter Benjamin on December 10, 1936, "If you're interested I can send a section of a story from the hospital that I wrote here. I've also started to translate a story about a contract-worker from Danish. It's really fun. You see, I've gotten over my laziness" (Hauck 221).[28] Curiously, Steffin self-denigrates her previous so-called laziness upon completing a work, instead of celebrating the accomplishment.

In 1936, Steffin married Danish citizen Svend Juul in order to receive national insurance. She was in the hospital from late 1939 to January 1940, when they had to move on to Sweden because of the Nazi takeover of Denmark. In Sweden, they decided to move to Helsinki and to arrange travel and visas for the United States. There the writer Hella Wuolioki invited them out to her farm in Marlebäck for the summer, where they had a better supply of food and where they could wait for the visas. Despite her worsening symptoms, Steffin wrote constantly in Finland; she took notes of Brecht's and Wuolioki's discussions and helped translate Wuolioki's stories. From October 1940 to May 1941, she typed the text for Brecht's and Wuolioki's play *Mr. Puntila and His Man Matti*, as well as *The Good Person of Sezuan* and *The Stoppable Rise of Arturo Ui*, the "Steffin collection" of Brecht's poetry, and the fragment from an English version of a Japanese play that Wuolioki had begun to revise, *Judith of Shimoda*. These eight months of Steffin's work—primarily as a secretary, Scribe Editorial, and typist—proved productive for Brecht and his enterprises, but not for Steffin's own.

The long-awaited visa arrived for Steffin in 1940, after Brecht and the others had received theirs, but Steffin's condition had worsened dramatically. Steffin's illness and drive to finish her work with Brecht drove her to nervous exhaustion. This text of a dream in January 1941 was an early birthday present for Brecht. Steffin dreamed of sailing on the "ship of fever" (Hauck 310), where the passengers are actors who demand more roles, and then demand that she choose her favorite play. She responded, "[A]ll the plays that have never seen a stage because of our times are my favorites! / 'Give them to us,' they scream . . . / 'But you can't perform them . . .' and I fall into water, I fall" (Hauck 313).[29] One must ask if this dream (or feverish delirium) perfectly revealed and encapsulated Steffin's frustration at taking a secondary role, at never having autonomously penned "all the plays that have never seen a stage," at not having fulfilled her potential as a writer, metaphorized by the fall into the water.

Because they waited so long for visas the Atlantic was no longer secure, so Brecht planned to travel to Moscow and on to Vladivostok, then by ship to California. Steffin wrote a last letter to her family to reassure them that they might not hear from her for months, and that no news would be good news (Reiber 343). In Moscow, Steffin was so weak that she had to be moved to the sanatorium. Steffin knew that time was of the essence, and selflessly urged Brecht to continue on to the United States. Brecht left her in the care of Maria Osten and the clinic staff, hoping that Steffin could revive and continue her journey. Steffin died at the age of 33 on June 4, 1941, the staff attending in her room, surrounded by manuscripts.

Conclusion

This study attempts to follow these two authors on their paths through their exile years and to shed some light on their experiences. United by their interest in Brecht, in socialism, and in Brecht's works, Hauptmann and Steffin had similar reactions to the stresses of exile even on different continents—initial excitement, then uncertainty and disappointment that their independence was limited by their legal status, their health, and their income. Their lack of self-confidence increased with each year until at one point they doubted even that they had written or could write: For Hauptmann it was doubt that she had spent so much time with Brecht writing. For Steffin it was doubt that she would be accepted, or could write without Brecht's input.

The political situation for Marxists and Communists, as well as the situation for women authors, left both dependent on a strong male figure for support and for opportunities to publish. Both Hauptmann and Steffin struggled to negotiate meeting their own needs and the needs of others, especially colleagues, as well as negotiating their reactions to insecurity, depression, and anxiety. Their story of becoming writers in their limited context, their disappointments and successes, as well as their continuing work with Brecht, is a story that fascinates even contemporary audiences. Their biographical and literary journeys left them in noncentral, nonautonomous roles but also proved them to be published writers, editors, and translators whose work was essential in Brecht's production of modern literary art.

Notes

1. From this point forward, all references to Brecht's collected works, the Berlin and Frankfurt edition, or *Berliner und Frankfurter Ausgabe,* will read "BFA," followed by file and page number.
2. "Sie erledigt alles, Karte, hiesiges Konsulat usw . . . fuer mich . . . Ich hatte mich zu Annahme dieser Einladung allerdings in einer Zeit entschlossen, als ich ziemlich verzweifelt war und auch das Verhalten von einigen Leuten, fuer die ich den Kopf hinhalten musste, sehr deprimiert hatte . . . Ich weiss auch nicht, ob es richtig ist, und auf jeden Fall braucht es ja nicht laenger als vier Monate zu sein." From this point forward, all references to *Elizabeth Hauptmann Archive* will read "EHA," followed by file and page number.
3. "Lassen Sie uns diese Art von Beziehung gänzlich abbrechen, Brecht. Sie sind anscheinend glücklich. Auch ich, das glauben Sie mir, werde bei *gänzlicherr* Trennung von Ihnen eine große selbstverständliche und sehr zärtliche Beziehung zu einem Menschen auch in der Arbeit, was ich mir wünsche, finden! Unsere Beziehung war etwas karg und unzärtlich und ungeschickt, aber es war die *g r ö ß t e* Arbeitsfreundschaft, die Sie je haben werden und die ich je haben werde . . . Ihre Bess

Hauptmann." From this point forward, all references to *Bertolt Brecht Archive* will read "BBA," followed by file and page number.

4. "Jetzt fange ich auch an zu verzweifeln, da ich so vieles vermisse. Hat sich bei Ihnen das 'Polly-bild' und die 'Ballade von der Billigung der Welt' eingefunden?"

5. "[E]rneuter Versuch, irgendein Loch (nicht im Zaun, sondern in den dicken Steinmauern) zu finden, durch das ich durchschlüpfen kann. Die Mauern sind aber meistens so gut instand und verzementiert, dass gar kein Spaeltchen zu entdecken ist. Allenthalben raet man mir, mich irgendwo hinzusetzen und einen Roman zu schreiben, dass ich waehrend des Schreibens schliesslich auch wo schlafen und essen muss, das interessiert (sicher mit Recht) niemanden."

6. "[D]ie Industrie finanziert die Kunst und die Künstler—die große Sonnabendnachmittagsaufführungen der Metropolitan Oper (die ein wahnsinniges Geld kosten) z.b. werden von den 'Lucky Strike' Zigarettenfabriken gesponsort—in den Pausen und hinterher wird der Text der Oper erzählt oder die Hauptdarsteller interview . . . es interessiert mich kolossal und nie hat mich die große nähe von Kunst und Geschäft so wenig gestört."

7. "[S]o moechte ich gern beteiligt sein mit dem Dreigroschensatz . . . Sie koennen es rubrizieren als Mitarbeiterbeteiligung oder als Vertriebsprovision. Ich waere mit der letzten Rubrizierung einverstanden, da ohne das nicht irgendwo hinten steht: im Anfang mitgeholfen hat E.H."

8. "Ich wünsche Ihnen alles alles Gute fuer 1935 Herzlichst Ihre Bess / Schreiben Sie doch mal, man ist hier naemlich wirklich sehr allein."

9. "Es ist genau ein Jahr, seitdem ich herkam und ist mir wie eine Ewigkeit. Schreiben Sie wieder. Ich möchte wissen, wie lange ich hier noch sitzen muss."

10. "Mein Gott, jetzt liegen schon Monate und fast Jahre zwischen jetzt und der Zeit, da ich Sie alle zuletzt sah. Ich weiss, dass, wenn nicht durch irgendwelche gluecklicheren Umstaende mein Schiff sich nicht bald wieder nach Europa wendet, ich dieses Land aus der Sicht verliere; schon jetzt geht mir das Gestruepp bis ueber die Augen und selbst manchmal, wenn ich gezwungen bin, . . . den Namen Brecht zu erwaehnen, ist es mir, als waere es ein Schwindel, dass ich mal jahrelang bis 18 Stunden taeglich mit ihm zusammen war, und mir entsinken die Worte, weil ich die Leute nicht beschwindeln moechte. Man fragte mich nach der *Maßnahme* und ploetzlich fiel mir in einer mir fremden Wohnung Augsburg ein, wo wir die japanische No-form transponierten die ersten Szenen vollbefriedigt an Ihering nach Berlin schickten zum Abdruck" (Haentzschel 179; from Theodor Adorno Archive, Frankfurt am Main, Germany, 5 Mar. 1935).

11. "Fuer mich is das Unterrichten am College noch immer hochinteressant. Ich habe einen ganzen Stab, der mit mir durch dick und dünn geht."

12. "Ich verdiene,—da es eine sogenannte FERA-Stellung ist, im Rahmen der Arbeitslosenbekämpfung—$45 im Monat. Davon gehen todsicher $5 Fahrgeld ab. Dabei darf ich keine an den Beinen gestopften Strümpfe tragen und mein Haar muss gepflegt sein. Ich darf nicht müde aussehen und muss nett angezogen sein. Der Grammatikunterricht muss interessant gemacht werden, wie eine Theatervorstellung."

13. "Liebe Beß, ich fahre also. Und hoffe, Du kommst bald nach. Es war sehr gut, daß Du mich in USA geführt hast—wie es immer vorgesehen war. Ich danke Dir sehr, liebe Beß. Und ich werde nichts vergessen. Ich werde Dich nicht für immer in St. Louis lassen. b / sobald ich in Dänemark bin werde ich die Sache drüben forcieren."

14. "[I]ch stellte ihm ganz bewußt geplante Fragen, mußte unendlich viel Bücher dazu nach lesen, und konsultierte auch noch andere Freunde, die in China gewesen waren . . . Die Memoiren sind also, was man so nennt, mein geistiges Eigentum . . . Auch [bei den Radiosendungen] war dein guter Vater begeistert von dem Plan, jede Woche übers Radio sprechen zu können . . . Aber wieder war er nicht zu bewegen, auch nur eine Zeile selber zu schreiben oder zu diktieren."

15. "Zwei Stunden für Brecht? Wer für Brecht arbeitet, arbeitet nicht unter vierundzwanzig Stunden am Tag!"

16. "Ich bin sehr froh, daß sie sich, zum ersten Mal wieder, doch meiner Arbeiten annimmt, sie ist unersetztlich."

17. "Zu versuchen, nicht ungeduldig zu werden, ist schwer. Zu versuchen, wenn man aelter geworden ist, ganz allein, d.h. ohne jede Beziehung, ohne ein paar einflussreiche Freunde durchzukommen, ist schwer . . . Es gibt fuer eine Frau ja nur 3 Loesungen: Entweder macht sie sich erotisch unentbehrlich. Oder sie macht sich arbeitsmaessig unentbehrlich. Oder sie blackmailed, wo das eine oder das andere nicht ausreicht. Dann gibt es das ganz andere, das klassifiziert dann die Frau nicht nur als Frau: sie macht sich ganz unabhängig und schafft sich ihre eigene einflussreiche Plattform."

18. "Ich rechne sehr damit, dass wir irgendein Arrangement treffen koennen und wieder zu Arbeit gelangen. Reden Sie sich nichts mit der Gesundheit ein, das ist nur eine Frage der Beschaeftigung. Sie sind ausgesehen, 90 Jahre alt zu werden und werden sich darueber noch oft beklagen . . . *Die Dreigroschenoper* soll Albers auf Tournee nehmen, das ist auch Geld [als Tantiemen] fuer Sie. Packen Sie also."

19. "Ich habe ein schlechtes Gewissen . . . Dabei war ich nicht mal faul. Aber der halbe Tag geht 'verloren' durch Behandlung, Essen, Mittagsruhe

von 2 Stunden usw . . . Mit den russischen Genossen spreche ich viel, vor allem versuche ich, ihre Ansichten zu hören über Frauenarbeit, über die Kirche und über Kinderarbeit."

20. "Heute träumte ich, dass ich bei dir läge."

21. "Schreien konnte ich nicht, weil ich so rannte / Doch da fuhrst du schon. Das Schlußlicht brannte. / Jetzt kommt nichts mehr, dacht ich. Und war still."

22. "Es ist bei Dir besonders schwer, ein Bild sich zu machen, obwohl (meiner nach die als erste wünschbare Verhaltensart) es gerade bei Dir leicht sein sollte besonders mit dir . . . (inbegriffen alle Freunde die ich kenne) jeder denkt dass sie dich kennen (oder dich kennen wollen) oder nicht: trotzdessen erwartet jeder 'eine Zigarette' von dir. Ich möchte das nicht. Das sollte nicht sein. Aber ich unterstelle: vielleicht—vielleicht ist nicht so?"

23. "[I]ch glaube, es ist unklug, zu warten, bis Du herkommst (DAD), das wird doch sicher sehr spät sein? Und bis dahin muss man wirklich angefangen haben . . . schlimm ist nur, dass alle die leute, die wir für uns hatten, langsam anfangen, andere korrespondenzen zu beliefern."

24. "[U]nd immer höre ich dann was helli zuletzt in berlin zu mir sagte; 'du tust mir leid, mein liebes kind.' dann tue ich mir selbst auch leid."

25. "Es wäre dies endgültig Schluß über 'diesen Komplex'. Außer nach-haltigen unangenehmen Zwischenfällen habe ich eine gute Erinner-ung an eine Zeit (diese Tage in Kopenhagen) in der Du ungeheuer nett u. rücksichtsvoll gegen mich warst. Daß Du es sein konntest, könnte mich zur Schuldnerin machen, aber ich bin 'eh'schon versklavt."

26. "[U]nd wenn ich auch verstehe, dass Du, zu hause" sein willst einige zeit, so stösst mir natürlich mächtig auf, dass ich kein 'zu hause' habe. nirgends. ich muss immer fur mich und meine koffer um einen platz bitten, und kann mir nicht mal bücher kaufen, weil wo soll ich sie hin-stellen? dann natürlich sehe ich immer ganz klar, es geht doch nicht. wenn Du dann auch so selten schreibst, was auch die gründe sind, so wird es in einem masse schlimm, wie ich es nicht sagen kann."

27. "Ich selbst möchte so furchtbar gern auch produktiv sein, aber ich muss Ihnen etwas gestehen: Immer, wenn ich etwas beginne, habe ich Angst, dass die Leute sagen werden, ich hätte es nicht selbst gemacht. Und deshalb höre ich wieder auf. Oder ich glaube, dass es nichts taugt."

28. "[W]enn es Sie interessierte, wuerde ich Ihnen mal einige auszuege ueber krankenhausberichte schicken, die ich hier gemacht habe. Sonst habe ich angefangen, einen tageloehner-roman aus dem daenischen zu uebersetzen. Es macht mir grossen spass. Sie sehen also, dass die faulheit sich ganz verzogen hat."

29. "Alle Stücke, die durch die Ungunst der Zeit nie eine Bühne gesehen, sie sind mir die liebsten! / Gib sie uns, schreien sie . . . / Ach ihr könnt sie nicht spielen! . . . / Und der schwankende Boden unter mir öffnet sich und ich falle, falle, falle."

Works Cited

Altman, Janet. *Epistolarity: Approaches to a Form*. Columbus: Ohio UP, 1982. Print.

Bentley, Eric. *The Brecht Memoir*. 2nd ed. Evanston: Northwestern UP, 1989. Print.

Bertolt Brecht Archive. Chausseestr. 125, Berlin.

Brecht, Bertolt. *Werke. Große Kommentierte Berliner und Frankfurter Ausgabe*. Ed. Werner Hecht et al. Berlin: Aufbau; Frankfurt au Main: Suhrkamp, 1988. Print.

———. *Briefe (Letters)*. Ed. Günter Glaeser. Vol. 1. Frankfurt au Main: Suhrkamp, 1981.

Gellert, Inge. *Margarete Steffin: Konfutze versteht nichts von Frauen: Nachgelassene Texte* (Berlin: Rowohlt, 1991). Print.

Küpper, Hannes, ed. *Der Scheinwerfer, Blätter der städtischen Bühnen Essens* (*The Spotlight, Journal of Essen City Stage*). 14 (1927–1933). N. pag. Print.

Eakin, Paul John. *How Our Lives Become Stories: Making Selves*. New York: Cornell UP, 1999.

Elisabeth Hauptmann Archive, Robert Koch Platz 10, D-10115, Berlin. Print.

Gross, Sabine. Rev. of *Briefe an berühmte Männer: Walter Benjamin, Bertolt Brecht, Arnold Zweig* (*Letters to Famous Men: Walter Benjamin, Bertolt Brecht, Arnold Zweig*). *Brecht Yearbook*. Vol. 26. 2001: 338–40. Print.

Haentzschel, Hiltrud. *Brechts Frauen*. Hamburg: Rowohlt, 2002. Print. Quotation of Hauptmann's letter to Benjamin, March 1935, from the Theodor Adorno Archive, Frankfurt au Main.

Hanssen, Paula. *Elisabeth Hauptmann: Brecht's Silent Collborator*. Bern: Peter Lang, 1995. Print.

Hauck, Stefan. *Margarete Steffin Briefe an Berühmte Männer: Walter Benjamin, Bertolt Brecht, Arnold Zweig*. Hamburg: Europäische Verlagsanstalt, 1999. Print.

Hauptmann, Elisabeth. *Julia ohne Romeo: Geschichten, Stücke, Aufsätze, Erinnerungen*. Berlin: Aufbau, 1977. Print.

Kebir, Sabine. *Ich fragte nicht nach meinem Anteil: Elisabeth Hauptmanns Arbeit mit Bertolt Brecht*. Berlin: Aufbau, 1997. Print.

Reiber, Hartmut. *Grüß den Brecht: Das Leben von Margarete Steffin*. Berlin: Eulenspiegel, 2008. Print.

Rubenstein, Roberta. *Home Matters: Longing and Belonging, Nostalgia and Mourning in Women's Fiction*. New York: Palgrave Macmillan, 2001. Print.

Steffin, Margarete. *Konfutze versteht nichts von Frauen, nachgelassene Texte*. Ed. Simone Barck. Berlin: Rowohlt, 1992. Print.

Willet, John. "Bacon ohne Shakespeare?—The problem of 'Mitarbeit.'" *Brecht, Women and Politics; The Brecht Yearbook* 12 (1985): 118–37.

2

A Lost Voice Remembered

María Teresa León's Triumph

Mary Thrond

Overview

María Teresa León was a Spanish writer at the forefront of political and intellectual activity during her country's civil war (1936–1939). Against all odds in twentieth-century Spain, her uncommon bravery and astute intellect allowed her to write prolifically and poetically about her political experience. After the Fascist defeat of the Republican democratic government, she was forced to flee Spain and spend nearly half her life in exile in France, Argentina, and Italy. Her lyrical and existential writing portrays the struggles of the women, children, workers, soldiers, intellectuals, and artists before, during, and after the war. Writing allowed her to discover her own voice, her literary identity, and the strength to combat the torment of exile. She artfully created an oral history that captures the voices of the fallen and forgotten, preserving the truth about the Republican experience, the experience Franco's repressive Fascist dictatorship had tried to censor and erase. By reconstructing her own experience in the Civil War and describing her anguish in exile she offered solace and hope to her fellow Spaniards, suffering from the same pain. As a Republican woman living in exile and writing in the shadow of her preeminent poet husband, María Teresa León might never have been appreciated were it not for the distinguishable style and complexity of her writing. Its resurgence in her beloved, free, and democratic Spain is a tribute to her poetic prose as well as to her relentless struggle for freedom.

"Pasará el tiempo. Pasaremos. Un día la tradición oral repetirá estas palabras sin saber el nombre de quien las escribió. Ese es el triunfo de un poeta."

The Spanish Civil War tore the people of Spain apart, leaving a gaping wound that would not heal. On July 18, 1936, the democratic government of the Spanish Republic was assaulted by an insurrection in its own military led by General Francisco Franco. A bloody civil war ensued, ending in 1939 with Franco's Fascist forces, the *nacionales,* defeating the government forces, the *republicanos.* Hundreds of thousands of Spaniards fled into exile. María Teresa León, a valiant Republican intellectual, was among those who escaped to France. She spent the next four decades in exile in France, Argentina, and Italy. Driven by a passion to write and an indefatigable commitment to the progressive ideals of the Republic, she portrayed the experiences of the fallen Republican forces and anguished exiles, like herself, in her writing.

She referred to writing as her *enfermedad incurable,* her "incurable disease" (8) in *Memoria de la melancolía (Memory of Melancholy).* It gave rise to her own voice, the lifeblood of her identity, and preserved the voices of her compatriots. María Teresa described how closely intertwined her life and her work were. "[I write anxiously, without] stopping, tripping, yet I go on. I go on because it is a form of breathing, without which I could die. I do not differentiate between living and writing" (*Memoria* 274–75).[1]

She embarked on her literary career by publishing articles in her hometown newspaper, *El Diario de Burgos,* in 1924. She did not even dare use her own name, opting to use the pseudonym Isabel Inghirami (*Memoria* 76). For the rest of her life she wrote articles, poems, essays, children's stories, plays, screenplays, translations, novels, and her extraordinary autobiography, *Memoria de la melancolía,* which is considered her masterpiece. Much of her lyrical prose and her moving memoirs portray the years of the Civil War and bemoan the years of exile. She captured the voices of the powerless, the heroic, the devastated, and the tormented. The young woman from Burgos who was too shy to sign her own name eventually became one of the most vibrant voices of the Spanish Republic.

Early Voices

Gregorio Torres Nebrera documents that María Teresa de Jesús Juana María del Rosario Lucila León y Goyri was born into a privileged, bourgeois family from Burgos on October 31, 1903 (15). Her father was a military officer and her mother was from an acclaimed literary family. María Teresa's aunt, María Goyri, wife of Spanish scholar Ramón Menéndez Pidal, was the first woman to graduate from and teach at a Spanish university (*Memoria* 62).

María Teresa was close to both of her parents. They, however, were very different from each other. Learning to understand these contrasts may have helped her learn to tolerate the ambiguities and contradictions that she encountered later in life. She described her parents and their differences in her autobiography. Fond of her father, she obviously cherished spending time with him: "I liked to go out with my father, to go to the horse races or to sit with him on the Ramblas. We were so happy when we went out to conquer the world together . . . They said that we looked alike" (*Memoria* 74).[2] Her mother's rebellious, unconventional nature and criticism of her father left its mark on María Teresa's personality and politics: "My mother did not believe very much in the Spanish army . . . Her intelligence refused to accept the glorious conquests . . . She had a response for everything. Her light blue eyes used to cloud over with rage. Why do men have to be so unintelligent? She would grab her *mantilla* and go off to pray . . . Later she grabbed her *mantilla* and went off to vote . . . She voted. She arranged her *mantilla* and went to church . . . to pray to God a little to give the Communist Party victory in the polls" (*Memoria* 74–75).[3] Thus the seed was planted for María Teresa to accept the dichotomies between leftist political ideology and conservative religious faith as well as between a feminist perspective and a masculine one. Living with her opinionated parents and their differences was not easy, however. She wrote about listening to their heated arguments in her memoirs: "The images have dissolved but not the voices . . . I cannot stand it . . . Only the voices have remained inside [me] . . . I do not want to hear my childhood" (*Memoria* 11–12).[4] This recollection of sounds is typical of her distinctive style. Her writing often evokes the senses of sound, smell, and sight.

She was a lonely child. Because of her father's military career her family had to move often. During her fairly isolated and uprooted childhood in Madrid, Barcelona, and Burgos, she developed a rebellious spirit. María Teresa recounted in her memoirs how she was expelled from the private Catholic school *Colegio del Sagrado Corazón* (Sacred Heart School) for reading the forbidden voices of Victor Hugo and Alexandre Dumas and aspiring to pursue higher education (*Memoria* 62–63). Inmaculada Monforte Gutiez observes that this experience was León's first encounter with established norms that did not allow her intellectual freedom (479).

In 1920, at the age of 17, María Teresa married a military man, Gonzalo de Sebastián Alfaro. They had two sons, Gonzalo and Enrique (Torres Nebrera 15). It was an unhappy marriage. Against Spanish society's norms, she decided to separate from her husband. He retaliated by denying her custody of their children. She was forced to make a mother's ultimate sacrifice for her independence. The loss of her sons caused her pain and sadness, yet she prevailed. She explained, "I had started to write because my days were long, cold and lonely" (*Memoria* 81).[5] Her suffering was the compelling force that moved her to write; developing her voice was the creative outlet for easing her sorrow.

María Teresa had been interested in writing from a young age. By the time of her first communion, her parents had sent her to visit the naturalist author Emilia Pardo Bazán. Pardo Bazán's compelling voice challenged the norms of Spanish society. She gave María Teresa her book *El tesoro de Galván* (*Galván's Treasure*) and wrote the following dedication: "To the young girl, María Teresa León, hoping that she follow the path of literature and the arts" (qtd. in Torres Nebrera 17; Estébanez Gil 43–44).[6] By encouraging her vocation, the established author fostered the development of María Teresa's young voice.

Developing her own voice and carving out her identity against the backdrop of conservative Spanish society was a daunting task for León. She turned to poetry for the support she needed to become the woman and the writer she aspired to be. She recalled, "In our family all of the women have been decent. All her life the girl closed her eyes when confronted with that threatening word of decency. She kept finding in poetry everything that life had insisted on denying her" (*Memoria* 42).[7] Between 1924 and 1928, she wrote nearly forty articles about feminist, cultural, and social issues for *El Diario de Burgos* (Torres Nebrera 17). She signed most of them with her pseudonym Isabel Inghirami (*Memoria* 76; Torres Nebrera 216). In his extensive bibliography, Torres Nebrera notes the emergence of her literary identity as she progressively replaced the pseudonym with her own name. First, he cites a January 1927 article signed simply "María Teresa." Later that same year, he notes an article signed "M.T." The articles published in late spring of 1928 were finally signed with her full name (216–17). Also in 1928, her first book, *Cuentos para soñar* (*Stories to Dream About*), a children's book, was published in Burgos. She signed it María Teresa León and dedicated it to her son Gonzalo (Estébanez Gil 43–44). Her writing had allowed her to begin discovering her voice, her literary identity, and to combat her suffering. It enabled her to preserve her own voice as a mother in order to read bedtime stories, albeit vicariously, to her children who had been taken from her.

Personal and Political Development

Disillusioned with life in Burgos, she moved to Madrid to seek independence and to further develop her intellect. There she quickly befriended the members of the literary and artistic circles of the Generation of '27. No woman writer was considered a member of the Generation of '27 although there were many intellectual women, like María Teresa León, who were writing with the same fervor as their male counterparts. María del Mar López-Cabrales offers an insight into the sociohistorical context to explain this phenomenon. Women had obtained suffrage and access to higher education, temporarily, during the Second Republic (1931–36). Nonetheless, the intellectual atmosphere remained conservative, sexist, and paternal. Women still needed their husbands' permission to publish and were limited to publications of minor distribution (López-Cabrales 177–79).

Marcia Castillo-Martín explains how in 1926 the women of Madrid fought back by establishing the Lyceum Club. It was based on the European Lyceum Clubs, centers for intellectual women, that many of them had visited in London. Founding the Lyceum acknowledged their ability to create their own realm, directed for and by them. These progressive and intellectual women were finally allowed to articulate their artistic and intellectual voices freely (Castillo-Martín16–17).

León recalled the courage and strength that this astute group of women had shown in establishing the Lyceum Club in the patriarchal Spanish society of that time: "The Lyceum Club was not a frivolous social gathering of women fanning themselves and dancing. In the drawing rooms . . . they conspired over lectures and cups of tea . . . The Lyceum Club was turning into the [back]bone of feminine independence that would be difficult to break. The Spanish clock had been moved ahead" (*Memoria* 334–35).[8]

Juan Carlos Estébanez Gil notes that some critics consider María Teresa León to be a member of the "women writers of the Generation of '27." This group, including Concha Méndez, Ernestina de Champourcín, Carmen Conde, and Josefina de la Torre, consisted of "educated women from families in good standing, who did not agree with the atmosphere they were living in; they sought their personal emancipation through their artistic and literary creation" (Estébanez Gil 45).[9] These women left a literary legacy that attests to their intellect and their courageous character.

María Teresa moved in the same social circles as the members of the Generation of '27 and also clearly chose politically leftist intellectuals as her closest friends and allies. She was friends with such celebrated Spanish authors as Rafael Alberti, Vicente Aleixandre, Luis Cernuda, Rosa Chacel, Concha Espina, Federico García Lorca, Miguel Hernández, Juan Ramón Jiménez, Antonio Machado, Pedro Salinas, and Miguel de Unamuno. She knew many writers from abroad like André Breton and André Malraux from France; Bertolt Brecht from Germany; Maxim Gorki and Boris Pasternak from Russia; John Dos Passos and Ernest Hemingway from the United States; Nicolás Guillén from Cuba; Pablo Neruda from Chile; Octavio Paz from Mexico; and Alfonsina Storni from Argentina. From the art world she was friendly with the leaders of the avant-garde movements of the 1920s: Pablo Picasso and the surrealists Joan Miró, Salvador Dalí, and Luis Buñuel (Estébanez Gil 57–58).

These associations made an impact on León's politics as well as on her writing. Politically and literarily, she clearly divided the world into the exploiters and the exploited (Marco 14). She took a firm stand supporting the Republic and her voice expressed its progressive political ideology. She shared in her memoirs, "Many times I have had to get up to talk from . . . a balcony . . . because the Spanish political atmosphere during those years obliged us to choose a clear position in our political conscience" (*Memoria* 50).[10]

In the days preceding the Spanish Civil War, she wrote her early work—for example, *Cuentos de la España actual* (*Stories from Contemporary Spain*)—in the social-realism style known as the "literature of urgency." Beverly Mayne Kienzle and Teresa Méndez-Faith define this style using Antonio Machado's words "*si mi pluma valiera tu pistola*" (if my pen were worth as much as your pistol) (323). Essentially, the writers hoped that their words would carry the same weight as firearms would to urge the Spanish people to stand up to the Fascist right-wing contingent of their society. After the war, influences of the avant-garde cubist and surrealist movements also appeared in León's work, notably in her polyphonic discourse and dreamlike narratives. Yet the strongest association to come from her early days in Madrid was that with the highly regarded Andalusian poet Rafael Alberti, who became her lifelong companion.

Life in Harmony with Alberti

In 1930, María Teresa León and Rafael Alberti met in a mutual friend's home. Alberti was reading from his work *Santa Casilda,* and León was the only one interested in discussing literature with him (Torres Nebrera 22). Thus began an intellectual bond, a political liaison, and a romantic relationship that would last more than fifty years. Inseparable from the start, they shared their travels, writing, political ideology, wartime activities, and time in exile together. They made a great impact on each other's work and life. López-Cabrales observes that one year after meeting her, Rafael denounced all his previous work as bourgeois poetry and decided to dedicate himself to writing revolutionary poetry. Shortly thereafter the couple joined the Communist Party together (179).

In December 1932, the couple embarked on a journey to the Soviet Union to study proletariat theater. There they met the revolutionary writers Kelyin, Fadiev, Gladkov, and Pasternak. Inspired by these contacts, they returned to Spain and founded *Octubre*, the official journal of the Revolutionary Writers and Artists organization (Torres Nebera 23–24). When the Civil War broke out, León and Alberti were leaders of the Republican intellectual forefront. In order to publish testimonials of the war by writers, soldiers, and factory workers, Francisco Caudet cites that they established another literary journal, *Mono Azul* (*Blue Coverall*), referring to the construction uniform worn by Republican men and women (43). These journals offered a venue to share the voices of the war-torn Spanish people.

During the war, León led the Alliance of Anti-Fascist Intellectuals and directed a theater troupe, *Las Guerrillas del Teatro* (*The Guerrillas of Theater*). Their theater performances reinforced the Republican political ideology and disseminated culture. The plays that León chose to perform were both classical and contemporary. Among others, she chose *La destrucción de Numancia* (*The Destruction of Numancia*), Alberti's version of *Numancia* by Cervantes; *El dragoncillo* (*The Little Dragon*) by Calderón; *Un duelo* (*A Duel*) by Chekhov; *Amor de don Perlimpín con Belisa en su jardín* (*Don Perlimpín's Love with Belisa in the Garden*) by García Lorca; and *Cantata de los héroes y la fraternidad de los pueblos* (*Cantata for Heroes and the Brotherhood of All People*) by Alberti (Estébanez Gil 278). In addition, León and Alberti collaborated with other intellectuals to save the treasures of Spain's artistic heritage. They organized the transportation of the masterpieces of the Prado Museum out of Madrid, safe from the Fascist bombings.

Years after the Civil War, Rafael described María Teresa's character in his own memoirs, *La arboleda perdida* (*The Lost Grove*): "She was very brave, as if her family name, León [*Lion*] protected her, giving her more courage" (Alberti 273).[11] Rafael recalled in *Mi vida con María Teresa León* (*My Life with María Teresa León*) how during the war, "she was a very courageous and very bold woman who often faced danger . . . She carried a pistol in her belt, regularly visited the frontlines and directed the Alliance of Anti-fascist Intellectuals and the Guerrillas of Theatre, performing plays near the trenches of the Republican troops. One day she even slapped the director of an organization against the war who tried to enter and seize the palace at 7 Marqués del Duero, the center of the Intellectual Alliance" (9).[12]

Exile

With the defeat of the Republican army and ensuing Fascist invasion of Madrid in 1939, María Teresa and Rafael were forced to flee Spain and seek refuge in France. They embarked on their long sojourn of exile by escaping in a small plane. Shirley Mangini reports that the Chilean Nobel Prize–winning poet Pablo Neruda offered them his home in Paris. They worked for a time with Radio France. When Hitler invaded France in 1940, General Franco asked for their extradition. They then fled by boat to the Americas and eventually settled in Argentina where they remained for 23 years (161).

They were well received in Argentina and joined many fellow Spanish exiles. This allowed them to reminisce and reflect on the Civil War from a distance. The birth of their daughter, Aitana, gave them hope for a new life in the Americas. They both wrote prolifically. Yet León and Alberti were not destined to live out their exile peacefully in Argentina. In the spring of 1963, the repression and censorship of Juan Perón's military government caused them to flee from Argentina and return to Europe (Loureiro 66). Once again, the political environment threatened to silence their voices and forced them to leave another country they had learned to call home.

Their next destination was Rome, which Monforte Gutiez observes "meant exhaustion, extreme fatigue and illness for León. The eternal flight weighs her down more as she ages and her mood is sad and melancholy . . . the constant fear of never returning to Spain is always on her mind" (478).[13] She prevailed nonetheless and finished writing her memoirs in Italy.

Dispelling Myths, Revising History

In exile, almost as a revisionist historiographer, León was committed to chronicling the truth about the Republican side of the war and to dispelling the myths about the Fascists. Both her nonfiction and her fiction keep the Republican version and vision of the war alive and expose the false voices of the Fascists. *Memoria de la melancolía,* her poetic autobiography, and *Juego limpio (Fair Play),* her lyrical historical novel, portray her wartime activities. She insisted on the need to retell the story: "Yes, the story must be told and retold so that those who listen to it know the price that this slice of still unfinished History, which occurred in a moment in Spain, cost" (*Memoria* 243–44).[14]

Driven by the passion for truth, León wanted to ensure that the Republican voices, which Franco's Fascist regime had censored and erased, be preserved for the Spanish people and for World History. *Juego limpio* is a riveting account of the final months of the war. She artfully created a fictional oral history of the resilient *republicanos* by narrating the events in the first person from multiple perspectives. She enhanced this literary technique by retelling the same scenes from different points of view. The resulting polyphonic effect makes the voices of the fallen and forgotten Republican heroes resonate more profoundly and vividly.

She was unabashed in her allegiance to the Republican cause and especially offended by the Fascists identifying themselves as the true patriots, the cultured bourgeoisie and ever-faithful Christians of Spain. Luis García Montero asserts that León did not want the world to forget about the origin of the war being the Fascist revolt (12). She wanted to clarify that the true patriots were those fighting in the Republican army, defending the Spanish government from the rebellious insurgents. She wanted it understood that although the Fascists called themselves the *nacionales,* they actually had revolted against the legitimately elected national government, the democratic Second Republic.

In her novel *Juego limpio,* León portrayed how the *republicanos* strove to educate the soldiers and to teach the illiterate to read. In contrast, the *nacionales* in the novel ridicule the *republicanos* for building schools with the money they had saved from the war. Furthermore, León makes the point that the Fascists had little or no regard for culture. They started the war by executing one poet, the internationally acclaimed Federico García Lorca. The war ended with another poet, Antonio Machado, dying, destitute in exile (*Juego limpio* 257).

The *nacionales* and their foreign allies, the German Nazis and the Italian Fascists, bombed Spain's cities relentlessly without regard for the Spanish people or their monuments and museums. Conversely, the *republicanos* carried out a well-documented rescue and relocation of the artistic treasures of the Prado Museum. While in exile, León wrote about this valiant effort to save cultural treasures from the rages of war. Her essay titled "La historia tiene la palabra: Noticia sobre el salvamiento del tesoro artístico" (History Has the Last Word: Information about Saving Artistic Treasure) was written for the Hispanic-Argentine Patronage of Culture in 1944 (Torres Nebrera 215). In essence, by documenting the Republican rescue effort she was prescribing the future protection of the artistic heritage of any nation at war. Photographs and documentation of the rescue effort were showcased in an exhibit at the Prado during the summer of 2003. The exhibit was titled "Arte Protegido: Memoria de la Junta del Tesoro Artístico durante la Guerra Civil" (Protected Art: A Record of the Committee for the Artistic Patrimony during the Civil War). It commemorated the role that León, Alberti, and their peers had played in the rescue.

León made a clear distinction between the foreign alliances from which the Fascists and Republicans sought support. The Fascists enlisted Hitler and Mussolini for bombing operations and soldiers from Morocco to commit barbarous acts; acts that the Fascist Spanish soldiers could not bring themselves to commit against their own countrymen. In contrast, the Republicans were supported by the International Brigade. The brigade was made up of foreign idealists who, García Montero notes, had come to "defender la legalidad de una nación asaltada por la barbarie [defend the legality of a nation attacked by barbarism]" (11).

Both León and Alberti paid tribute to the International Brigade in their art. Alberti wrote the play *Cantata de los héroes y la fraternidad de los pueblos* (*Cantata for Heroes and the Brotherhood of All People*) and León recited the role of "Spain" on stage for their official farewell. Her performance was so memorable that in 1990, Spanish film director Carlos Saura directed the actress Carmen Maura to reenact it in his celebrated film *¡Ay Carmela!*, based on Sanchis Sinisterra's 1986 play (Torres Nebrera 159). *Juego limpio* can be considered León's own "Cantata for Heroes" for the International Brigade as well as for the Republican forces.

Finally, the Catholic Church wholeheartedly supported Franco and the Fascist forces. The *nacionales* claimed to have God on their side. Regardless, León makes the point that this did not mean that the *nacionales* were all true believers nor that the *republicanos* were all atheists. In her memoirs, she cited some examples of the sanctimonious Church's indiscretions. She learned that bishops had blessed cannons. She had seen photographs of clergy saluting the insurgent *nacionales* with the raised-arm Fascist salute (*Memoria* 244). She recounted reports of priests slapping condemned Republican prisoners because they refused to confess their sins before dying (247). León succinctly demonstrated the Republican tolerance and respect for religion in *Juego limpio*. Her choice of a Catholic priest who converts to the Republican cause as the protagonist enabled her to distinguish between religious faith and the hierarchy of the Church. In an ongoing inner monologue, Camilo, the young priest, makes several revealing statements regarding this distinction: "*No creo en sus razones de orden, jerarquía, de tradición*" (I do not believe in its reasons for order, hierarchy, and tradition) (*Juego Limpio* 21); "*fui . . . capaz . . . de encontrar el equilibrio entre su fe y mi fe*" (I was . . . able . . . to find the balance between its faith and mine) (31); "*Dios mío . . . Jamás te he abandonado*" (My God . . . I have never forsaken you) (53). León wrote herself into the novel as the secretary of the Alliance of Anti-Fascist Intellectuals. While carrying their dead comrade Gerda Taro, the secretary noticed one of the theater troupe's actresses secretly making the sign of the cross. She urged her to go ahead without trying to hide her gesture out of shame (125; *Memoria* 183–85).

In another incident, Claudio, one of the main characters of *Juego limpio*, describes the evacuation of a convent that the Republicans needed to use. The nuns were terrified because of the Republican reputation for murdering nuns and priests. Claudio tried to explain to them that there was nothing to fear. He told them that it was Franco's fault that they had to be taken out of their tranquil setting. Franco was responsible for dividing up the Spanish people and for so many of them dying. Franco was protecting the Church, yet allowing the clergy and nuns to become martyrs. The nuns were taken to the Republic's legendary spiritual leader, Dolores Ibárruri, "*La Pasionaria*," to be given refuge in another convent. Later, Claudio commented to himself that he was sure that the truth about this rescue would not be reported. He knew "[Radio Sevilla] would continue to confuse us with others . . . , calling us young barbarians, rapists of nuns" (156).[15]

The Redemptive Voice from Exile

In María Teresa León's lyrical and existential writing she captured the experience of civil war and exile. She accomplished much more, however. She poetically preserved history, reconstructed the collective identity of the exiled, and provided hope for a peaceful, democratic Spain in the future. Relentlessly, she tried to reconstruct her own life throughout the years spent in exile.

As her anguish persisted, so did her passion to record it. Mangini notes that exiles need to write "from both personal and moral necessity" (159). She cites the introduction to Concha Méndez's memoirs, written by Méndez's granddaughter, Paloma Ulacia Altolaguirre: "One of the characteristics of the exiles is . . . the sensation that their identity has been lost—which is the reason why their memories become doubly important. Since they have lost the context in which they had evolved, the need to remember surpasses the limits of simple nostalgia converting itself into the spinal cord of the identity" (158).

The need to remember, in fact, and recording those memories, was essential to María Teresa, more so than her very survival. She recalled how while she was growing up, someone used to say, "One must have memories. Living is not as important as remembering. The horrifying thing would be not having anything to remember" (*Memoria* 54).[16] Her writing was her lifeblood, and its survival was integral to her being remembered. In her memoirs she reflected on her desire to be remembered by her fellow Spaniards: "I do not know if those who stayed behind or who were born later realize that we are Spain's exiled. We are who they will become once the truth of liberty is reestablished. We are the dawn that they are awaiting . . . , we are Spain's banished, those who seek the shadows, the silhouette, the sound of silent steps, the lost voices" (*Memoria* 31).[17]

Most of León's work was published in exile, in Mexico and in Argentina. It was banned in Spain and only released there after Franco's death in 1975. Regarding this body of work, Susana Rodríguez Moreno forewarns, "To delve into the literature that María Teresa León wrote during exile is to embark on a dense and profound journey, rich in discourse, yet torturous. After all, it is the personal history of a literary exile" (349). She goes on to state, "[T]he creative process requires a strong commitment and constitutes a form of struggle against forgetting" (351–52).[18]

The experience of being in exile affected both the content and the style of the exiled writers. León wrote in polyphonic discourse and randomly ordered chronology. María Carmen Riddel notes that her literary techniques "contribute to clearly mark the various stages of life: before and over there, here and now, everyday life and political activity" (43).[19] Alternating between first and third person, past and present, Madrid and Rome, León poignantly described her struggle to reconcile her identity in her memoirs: "[T]hat young woman who crossed Alcalá Street on the arm of a poet . . . always has a hard time realizing that she lives on the street of banishment . . . She just cannot seem to put the two parts of her heart together" (35).[20]

As León struggled to come to grips with the complexities and ambiguities of her identity, so, too, did other exiles. The Spanish scholar and son of an exiled Spaniard, Michael Ugarte accounts for this struggle for identity by describing the dynamics of such a transitory existence: "In exile, life ends, yet it continues; the effect is that the self is split by a notion of temporality which allows the present self to inspect and re-create the former one, to give it a new birth" (82). A Spanish exile, Adolfo Sánchez Vázquez, described the torment of this struggle: "[T]he memory of what had existed individually and collectively . . . could not be turned off; remembering it is like an open wound that cannot seem to heal itself" (23).[21] León tried to heal that wound for herself and her fellow exiles through her writing.

Mangini regards León as "clearly the most poetic memory text writer" because of her "conscious artistry" and the "raw emotion" with which she writes the "collective testimony" of the masses of Spaniards who were forced into exile (162). Availing herself of Mikhail Bakhtin's research on feminist autobiography, Riddel asserts that León's polyphonic discourse displaces individualism and creates an existential identity, composed of an accumulation of life experiences (44). Furthermore, Ángel Loureiro proposes that readers of autobiography can ideally reach a better understanding of themselves from the self-reconstruction of the autobiographer (xi–xvi). León relentlessly tried to reconstruct her own life throughout exile, offering solidarity and compassion to the exiled, who struggled to heal their emotional scars.

By revising history to include the Republican experience, she recognized the valiant efforts of the fallen, validated their experience and offered them solace. Estébanez Gil notes how León "treats the theme of anonymous and collective characters in the context of war, rebelling against the treatment of traditional history,"[22] and goes on to assert that "[t]he people who unite around revisionist history create the hope needed to reconstruct their lost native land" (58–59).[23] In her memoirs, León offered hope to her comrades in exile, recognizing their anguish and suffering: "We are those who are left, consumed by our passion for the truth. I know that the world barely hears us . . . The only route that we, Spain's banished, have not taken is that of resignation . . . Happy are the people who can recover as many times as they need to in order to survive" (*Memoria* 8).[24]

"Triumph of a Poet"

As a Republican woman living in exile and writing in the shadow of her preeminent poet husband, María Teresa León might never have been appreciated in Spain were it not for the distinguishable style and complexity of her writing. Her work weaves an intricate tapestry that portrays the struggles of women, children, soldiers, workers, intellectuals, and artists before, during, and after the war. Its resurgence in her beloved, free, and democratic Spain is as much a credit to its literary eloquence as it is a tribute to the struggle for liberty.

Academia has the responsibility to research exiled writers and recognize their work in order to incorporate it into the mainstream curriculum. León's poetic prose deserves to be included in anthologies of Spanish, feminist, and twentieth-century literature. Her autobiography, *Memoria de la melancolía,* and her novel *Juego limpio,* merit recognition as uniquely poignant testimonials to the same nightmarish reality that Picasso's painting *Guernica* portrays. León and Picasso both attest to the horrors of the Spanish Civil War, in particular, and to war in general in an innovative, avant-garde style.

María Teresa León referred to herself as "*la cola del cometa*" (the tail of the comet) (*Memoria* 122), trailing along behind the light of her husband, Rafael. In truth, her work was largely unrecognized during her lifetime, overshadowed by Rafael's luminary fame. Yet ironically, when Rafael drew a portrait of her for a posthumous tribute, he portrayed her as a celestial being with his signature entangled in her long flowing hair, positioning himself as the tail and León as the comet.

María Teresa wrote, "Time will pass. We will pass. One day the oral tradition will repeat these words without knowing the name of the one who wrote them. That is the triumph of a poet" (*Memoria* 316).[25] The recent resurgence of publication and celebration of her lyrical prose in Spain, the reenactments of her dramatic performances in film and theater, and the exhibit in the Prado Museum, reaffirm that her poetic voice has indeed triumphed and achieved her goal of preserving the truth about the Republican experience.

Tragically, while finishing her memoirs in Rome, María Teresa began to suffer the effects of Alzheimer's disease. She was painfully aware of the toll that the dreaded disease was taking on her. Once again she demonstrated her courage and her introspective intellect: "I am afraid to look at myself in mirrors because I don't see anything in my pupils and . . . , I don't know why they insist so in reviving my memory . . . I suffer from forgetting" (*Memoria* 19).[26] A cruel twist of fate was robbing her of her memory, her voice, and her identity.

Franco's repressive dictatorship eventually came to an end with his death in 1975. After the legalization of the Communist Party in April 1977, María Teresa León and Rafael Alberti returned to Madrid. The sad irony is that when she finally returned to Spain, because of the extent of the effects of Alzheimer's disease, León did not even realize that she had come home to a modern Spanish democracy. Estébanez Gil made the observation that "[h]aving overcome her geographic exile, she could not overcome the mental exile that Alzheimer's disease imposed upon her" (55–56).[27] Yet suffering from the disease as she was, "[the first thing she insisted on was] to visit her old neighborhood in Madrid" (59).[28] Her condition deteriorated and she spent her last years in oblivion in a geriatric clinic (Torres Nebrera 59).

In his 1989 tribute Salvador Arias, an actor from *The Guerillas of the Theater*, provided a testimonial to María Teresa León's resilient artistic spirit. He shared an anecdote of the last time he had visited her in the clinic. After making several futile attempts to jog her memory he decided to ask her if she liked the theater. He described her reaction: "Those little blue eyes, that were almost inexpressive at the time, sparkled for a second. She lifted her head and looked at me and then in a soft voice she whispered, quietly but firmly, 'Of course!' as a last testament to what the theater had meant to her in her lifetime" (75).[29] Not even disease could break her spirit entirely nor silence her voice completely.

María Teresa León died in the winter of 1988 at the age of 85 from the physical deterioration caused by Alzheimer's disease (Estébanez Gil 15). On December 14, 1988, the cold day that she was laid to rest, a general strike had been called, and the streets of Madrid were filled with people in political protest—an unintentional tribute to León, one of the foremost writers and political activists of the time (Torres Nebrera 60). The relentless chants and raised banners were testimony to the freedom that she had poetically defended throughout her lifetime. Not even her own death could silence the echo of her indomitable voice.

Notes

1. "deterneme, tropiezo pero sigo. Sigo porque es una respiración sin la cual sería capaz de morirme. No establezco diferencias entre vivir y escribir."
2. "Me gustaba salir con mi padre, ir a las carreras de caballos, sentarme con él en las Ramblas. Éramos tan felices cuando nos íbamos juntos a conquistar el mundo . . . Decían que nos parecíamos."
3. "Mi madre no creía mucho en el ejército español . . . Su inteligencia se negaba a aceptar las glorias derrotas . . . tenía una respuesta para todo. Sus claros ojos azules se enturbiaban de rabia. ¿Por qué los hombres serán tan poco inteligentes? Agarraba la mantilla y se iba a rezar . . . Más tarde, agarró la mantilla y se fue a votar . . . Votó. Arregló su mantilla y se fue a la iglesia . . . fue a rezar un poco para que Dios diera el triunfo al Partido Comunista."
4. "Se han disuelto las imágenes pero no las voces . . . No puedo sorportarlo . . . Las voces solas se han quedado dentro. No quiero oír mi infancia."
5. "[H]abía empezado a escribir porque mis días eran largos, fríos y solos."
6. "A la niña María Teresa León, deseándola que siga el camino de las Letras."
7. "En nuestra familia todas las mujeres han sido decentes. La niña cerró sus ojos ante aquella palabra amenazadora de decencia para toda la vida. En la poesía iba encontrando todo lo que tan insistentemente le había negado la vida."

8. "El Lyceum Club no era una reunión de mujeres de abanico y baile. En los salones . . . se conspiraban entre conferencias y tazas de té . . . El Lyceum Club fue convirtiendo en el hueso difícil de romper de la independencia femenina. Se había propuesto adelantar el reloj de España."

9. "[M]ujeres de buenas familias, educadas e inconformes con el ambiente en que vivían, que buscaron su emancipación personal a través de su creación artística y literaria."

10. "Muchas veces he tenido que subir a hablar . . . a un balcón . . . porque los tiempos españoles de aquellos años nos hicieron tomar una posición clara en nuestra conciencia política."

11. "Ella era muy valiente, como si su apellido—León la defendiera, dándole más arrestos."

12. "[E]ra una mujer muy valiente, muy audaz, que corrió muchos peligros . . . Llevaba una pistola al cinto, iba al frente, dirigía la Alianza de Intelectuales Antifascistas y Las Guerrillas del Teatro, haciendo teatro al borde de las trincheras republicanas. Un día, hasta dio bofetadas a un jefe de una organización llamada la Contraguerra que intentó entrar e incautar el palacio en Marqués del Duero número 7, el centro de la Alianza de Intelectuales."

13. "[S]ignificaba para León el cansancio, el agotamiento y la enfermedad. La eterna huida le pesa más con los años y su perspectiva es triste y melancólica . . . el miedo de no regresar a España está constantemente en su pensamiento."

14. "Sí, hay que contar y recontar la historia para que los que la escuchen sepan el precio que costó ese trozo de Historia inacabada aún en un momento de España."

15. "[Radio Sevilla] sigue confundiéndonos . . . , llamándonos jóvenes bárbaros, violadores de monjas."

16. "Hay que tener recuerdos. Vivir no es tan importante como recordar. Lo espantoso era no tener nada que recordar."

17. "No sé si se dan cuenta los que quedaron por allá, o nacieron después, de quiénes somos los desterrados de España. Nosotros somos ellos, lo que ellos serán cuando se restablezca la verdad de la libertad. Nosotros somos la aurora que están esperando . . . Nosotros somos los desterrados de España, los que buscamos la sombra, la silueta, el ruido de los pasos del silencio, las voces perdidas."

18. "Adentrarse en la obra literaria de María Teresa León escrita durante su exilio es iniciar un camino denso, profundo, rico en multiplicidad de registros pero también tortuoso. Pues, es la historia de un destierro literario . . . [L]a creación comporta un compromiso y una forma de lucha contra el olvido."

19. "[C]ontribuyen a marcar muy claramente las varias instancias de vida: el antes y el allá, el aquí y el ahora, la vida familiar y la actividad política."

20. "[A] aquella mujer joven que cruzó la calle de Alcalá del brazo de un poeta . . . le cuesta siempre darse cuenta de que vive en la calle del destierro . . . No consigue unir las dos partes de su corazón."

21. "[L]a memoria de lo que existió individual y colectivamente . . . , no puede cerrarse; su recuerdo es como una herida abierta que no logra cicatrizarse."

22. "[T]rata el tema de los personajes anónimos o colectivos en el contexto de la guerra en rebelión al tratamiento histórico tradicional."

23. "El pueblo unido a la intrahistoria crea la esperanza para reconstruir la patria perdida."

24. "Somos los que quedamos gentes devoradas por la pasión de la verdad. Sé que en el mundo apenas se nos oye . . . El único camino que no hemos hecho los desterrados de España es el de la resignación . . . Feliz el pueblo que puede recuperarse tantas veces para sobrevivir."

25. "Pasará el tiempo. Pasaremos. Un día la tradición oral repetirá estas palabras sin saber el nombre de quien las escribió. Ese es el triunfo de un poeta."

26. "Me asusta mirarme a los espejos porque ya no veo nada en mis pupilas y . . . , no sé por qué ponen tanta insistencia en reavivarme la memoria . . . sufro por olvidar."

27. "Superado el exilio geográfico, no pudo superar el exilio mental al que la sometió el mal de Alzheimer."

28. "[Lo primero en que insistió fue] visitar su antiguo barrio madrileño."

29. "Aquellos ojitos azules, entonces ya casi inexpresivos, chispearon un segundo, levantó la cabeza, me miró y también muy bajo, pero casi con firmeza, murmuró un rotundo '¡Claro!' como un último testimonio de lo que el teatro significó en su vida."

Works Cited

Alberti, Rafael. *La arboleda perdida*. 1959. Valencia: Círculo de Lectores, 1975. Print.

———. "Mi vida con María Teresa León." *Homenaje a María Teresa León*. Madrid: Universidad Complutense, 1990. 9–11. Print.

Arias, Salvador. "Testimonio." *Homenaje a María Teresa León*. Madrid: Universidad Complutense, 1990. 65–73. Print.

Arte protegido: Memoria de la Junta del Tesoro Artístico durante la guerra civil. Madrid: El Museo del Prado, 2003. Print.

Caudet, Francisco. "El *Mono Azul* y el *Romancero de la Guerra Civil.*" *Anthropos* 148 (1993): 43. Print.

Estébanez Gil, Juan Carlos. *María Teresa León: Estudio de su obra literaria.* Burgos: La Olmeda, 1995. Print.

García Montero, Luis. "La pasión de la memoria." Preface. *Juego limpio.* By María Teresa León. Madrid: Visor Libros, 2000. 7–18. Print.

León, María Teresa. *Una estrella roja.* Madrid: Espasa-Calpe, 1979. Print.

———. *Juego limpio.* 1959. Madrid: Visor Libros, 2000. Print.

———. *Memoria de la melancolía.* 1970. Barcelona: Editorial Laia, 1977. Print.

López-Cabrales, María del Mar. "Tras el rostro/rastro oculto de las mujeres en la generación del 27." *Letras Femeninas* 24.1–2 (1998): 173–87. Print.

Loureiro, Ángel G. *The Ethics of Autobiography: Replacing the Subject in Modern Spain.* Nashville: Vanderbilt UP, 2000. Print.

Mangini, Shirley. *Memories of Resistance: Women's Voices from the Spanish Civil War.* New Haven: Yale UP, 1995. Print.

Marco, Joaquín. Preface. *Una estrella roja.* By María Teresa León. Madrid: Espasa-Calpe, 1979. 9–23. Print.

Mayne Kienzle, Beverly, and Teresa Méndez-Faith. *Panoramas literarios: España.* New York: Houghton, 1998. Print.

Monforte Gutiez, Inmaculada. "María Teresa León a través de la memoria." *Sessenta anos depois: Os escritores do exilio republicano: Actas do congreso 16, 17, e 18 de marzo de 1999.* Ed. X. L. Axeitos and C. Portela Yánez. La Coruña: Edicios do Castro, 1999. 475–82. Print.

Riddel, María Carmen. "Última etapa del exilio de María Teresa León: La escritura reparadora." *Donaire* 14 (2000): 38–46. <http://www.sgci.mec.es./uk/Don/Don14/riddle.PDF>.

Rodríguez Moreno, Susana. "El mundo literario en el exilio de María Teresa León: *Memoria de la melancolía.*" *El exilio literario español de 1939.* Ed. Manuel Aznar Soler. Vol. 1. Barcelona: Gexel, 1998. 349–55. Print.

Sánchez Vázquez, Adolfo. "Entre la memoria y el olvido." Preface. *El exilio literario español de 1939.* Ed. Manuel Aznar Soler. Vol. 1. Barcelona: Gexel, 1998. 23–27. Print.

Torres Nebrera, Gregorio. *Los espacios de la memoria: La obra literaria de María Teresa León.* Madrid: Ediciones de la Torre, 1996. Print.

Ugarte, Michael. *Shifting Ground. Spanish Civil War Exile Literature.* Durham: Duke UP, 1989. Print.

3

An Argentine in Paris

The House of Memory: Exile in Alicia Dujovne Ortiz's *El árbol de la gitana*

Kimberle S. López

Overview

In her autobiographical novel El árbol de la gitana *(1997), Argentine author Alicia Dujovne Ortiz narrates her political exile during the 1976–83 "Dirty War" in which tens of thousands of Argentine citizens were persecuted by their country's military dictatorship. Although Paris has long been a preferred destination for Latin American writers, Dujovne Ortiz's narrator, Alicia, struggles with the difficulty of establishing a home in France. Drawing on Gaston Bachelard's* Poetics of Space, *in which the narrator is portrayed as reading during the course of the novel, this essay develops the notion of how as an exile herself, but also as the granddaughter of immigrants, the protagonist seems to feel that a real home is beyond her reach and instead relies on her family history to construct a "house of memory."*

"But then, can you imagine a more pleasant place of exile . . . than Paris?"

—Breyten Breytenbach,
"A Letter from Exile, to Don Espejuelo" 13

"Paris is clearly the most favored modern island of exile, but it is difficult to take seriously the punishment which sends you there."

—William Gass, "Exile" 217

Argentine author Alicia Dujovne Ortiz's autobiographical fiction *El árbol de la gitana* (1997) tells the story of the narrator Alicia's exile in France during the period of repression known as the Dirty War (1976–1983) in which some thirty thousand Argentine citizens were "disappeared"—that is, kidnapped, tortured, and murdered by the military government. Following the dictatorship, there was at first a great deal of public interest in remembering and documenting the cases, but soon the tide turned toward forgetting in the name of moving forward with national healing. Due to this historical context, the theme of memory is of particular importance in Argentine writing of recent decades. The story develops through Alicia's conversations with an enigmatic gypsy woman who appears to her periodically throughout the novel. Exiled in France, she draws on her own memory and that of her ancestors to construct a sense of home.

One of the results of the Dirty War was that it divided Argentines into two groups: those who left, and those who stayed. Curiously, both exiles and those who remained in the country believed they had a privileged perspective on Argentine culture and were preserving the true national patrimony. Outside their own country, exiles were able to publish without fear of censorship and enjoyed the perspective afforded by a critical distance from the regime, enhanced by access to international news about human rights violations. Thus many exiles considered themselves the guardians of an authentic Argentine identity that needed to be safeguarded when they were outside their country during the dictatorship. Those who remained at home considered that only they had the authority to represent national identity, since they had the immediacy of experiencing life in the homeland during those years firsthand. They believed that "one word written in Argentina was equal to rivers of ink spilled abroad" (Sarlo 102). Alicia Dujovne Ortiz describes this rift in her advice manual for émigrés, *Al que se va* (*For the One who Leaves*), where she refers to a divided Argentina in which the two groups "competed on the basis of suffering and conscience, running a race whose prize consisted in determining who had understood best and whom had been hurt worst" (16).

Regarding the question of who has suffered most, exiles in Paris—to which group Dujovne Ortiz herself belongs—were the least likely to inspire sympathy among both those who remained in Argentina under the dictatorship and exiles in other parts of the world. At least since the middle of the nineteenth century, Paris has been the cultural capital held up by Argentine writers and statesmen as a model that Buenos Aires should aspire to emulate; a favored destination for affluent Southern Cone travelers; an educational center where young men and women of South America aim to complete their studies; and an intellectual hub where publishing decisions with repercussions throughout the Western World are made.

As sociologist Margarita del Olmo observes, "Europe for Argentines mostly means France, the most important cultural reference" (116). Along parallel lines, in their study of exiles in France, Ana Vásquez and Ana María Araujo assert that for South American exiles, France *is* Europe (15). And as the film *Tangos: El exilio de Gardel* describes, Paris is the "capital of all exiles."

If Paris is considered "the cultural capital of Europe" (Kramer 12) throughout the Western World, it is particularly idealized by Southern Cone writers. Because of its cultural prestige, "Paris is *the* international literary capital to many Latin American urban intellectuals" (Schwartz 18). And as Vásquez and Araujo state, "Exile or not, the fact of coming to Europe, the fact of living in Paris, for a Latin American intellectual, is an achievement, a privilege" (164). Traditionally, for artists or art forms to be valorized in Argentina, they first had to be recognized in France. Thus for the Southern Cone intelligentsia, travel or study in Europe, and specifically France, has long been perceived as a rite of passage, considered a prerequisite for understanding not only other cultures but notably one's own national identity. In his memoirs, exiled Peruvian writer Alfredo Bryce Echenique eloquently depicts Paris as a formative locus where Latin Americans learn about themselves and learn to become writers. As Dujovne Ortiz remarks in *Buenos Aires*, "Where else could I go, other than Paris?" (104). Thus in *El árbol de la gitana*, when it becomes apparent that the narrator must seek exile along with her 13-year-old daughter, she wonders, "Where shall we go?" Her gypsy interlocutor replies, without hesitation, "To Paris" (17). Clearly Paris is the only logical destination for an exiled writer.

Dujovne Ortiz describes the French capital as the equivalent of Mecca for residents of Buenos Aires: "Going to Paris is the natural fulfillment, the *only* fulfillment, of the existence of those from Buenos

Aires . . . One says, in Buenos Aires, that the stork brings babies . . . from Paris. We return then to Paris, as one returns to one's source" (*Buenos Aires* 104). Dujovne Ortiz repeats a national saying: "When a good Argentine dies, he goes to Paris" (*María Elena Walsh* 124); thus Paris is the ultimate origin, the place where life begins and ends. Consequently, exile in France can be perceived less as a displacement to a foreign land, and more as a homecoming: "Going to Paris for us is a return" (*Buenos Aires* 104). Alicia Dujovne Ortiz is the granddaughter of immigrants to Argentina. Argentina has often been called a "country of immigrants," whose late twentieth-century exiles engage in what she calls a "reverse immigration" back to Europe (*Al que se va* 11, 48). Because of the cultural cachet associated with Paris, the City of Lights, it is hard for their Argentine countrymen to feel sorry for them. They describe them, disparagingly, as "self-sacrificing drinkers of champagne who chew the harsh caviar of exile" 16).

Exiles in Paris inspire little sympathy on the part of their compatriots, but exiled writers inspire the least of all. France is a privileged locale where intellectuals can potentially establish a more prestigious career than they can at home and can return home later enriched by the experience. As Vásquez and Araujo affirm, Paris is "a privileged place of artistic creation" (16), the enviable site where Latin American intellectuals aspire to live, and, after a period of adjustment, where they can begin to make their living by writing and publishing (176). In the wake of the Dirty War, Dujovne Ortiz's narrator, a writer like the author herself, has the mobility to live in Paris and travel to Argentina, but she never quite feels at home in either place.

The Poetics of Space in *El árbol de la gitana*

"The homeland, that place where I am not"

—Fernando Pessoa, cited in Benedetti, *Andamios* 50

"Abroad, where the only homeland is memory"

—Alicia Dujovne Ortiz, *El árbol de la gitana* 220–21

El árbol de la gitana is an autobiographical novel tracing the family tree of the narrator, Alicia, who bears the same name as the author, Alicia Dujovne Ortiz. Alicia (the author) was born in Buenos Aires in 1939. Her literary production began in the 1960s and consists of early collections of poetry and, more recently, numerous novels, essays, and biographical and autobiographical works, many of which were published first in French and later in Spanish. In 1978 she left Argentina for France as a political exile, at a time when many of her friends had been "disappeared," and her newspaper editor, Jacobo Timerman, had been tortured and imprisoned. At this juncture, the author feared for her own safety and that of her 13-year-old daughter, in light of the fact that her late father, a founding member of Argentina's Communist Party, had been imprisoned for subversion and had edited for his Communist press books that were now being burned by the military regime. Following the 1983 redemocratization, Dujovne Ortiz began returning to Argentina for periodic visits, and her nostalgia was so great that in 1999 she moved back; in 2002, however, she returned to France as part of a new wave of economically motivated exiles (*Al que se va* 15–17).

In terms of narrative structure, *El árbol de la gitana* is composed of alternating chapters that intertwine the story of the protagonist's exile in France with tales the elusive gypsy woman tells her about her ancestors. Alicia's family on both sides is composed of Old World immigrants: Western European Catholics on her mother's side and Eastern European Jews on her father's. Recognizing that in her situation as an exile and as the descendant of immigrants her only homeland is memory, the protagonist reconstructs her own sense of home in the roots that can be found in her family tree. With the aid of her gypsy interlocutor, the first-person narrator takes us on a journey from the time of Christopher Columbus through diverse waves of immigration and into the late twentieth century when Alicia opts for exile in France over oppression in Argentina.

In this autobiographical fiction, we see the exiled narrator living in various different situations in France, all of them temporary. In the chapters set in the contemporary period, Alicia, in her living arrangements, oscillates between a series of apartments in Paris and a succession of castles in the French countryside. As scholars observe, home is not just a space but a combination of a time and a space (Douglas 263; Gurr 11; Siedel 163). As a result, in *El árbol de la gitana*, the function of memory in the construction of real and imagined domiciles is critical to the narrator's sense of self.

Significantly, on one train trip back to the city, Alicia is portrayed as reading *The Poetics of Space* by French philosopher Gaston Bachelard. As Bachelard observes, "On whatever theoretical horizon we examine it, the house image would appear to have become the topography of our intimate being" (xxxii). In *El árbol de la gitana*, Dujovne Ortiz peers into the nooks and crannies of the exile's psyche by describing in detail the various temporary households in which the protagonist dwells.

An analysis of the influence of Bachelard's *Poetics of Space* on Dujovne Ortiz's thinking sheds light on the representation of home in her autobiographical narrative. Notably, the vacillation between castles and apartments would be interpreted by Bachelard as a manifestation of a human need for both warm, cozy spaces and bright, open spaces: "When we live in a manor house we dream of a cottage, and when we live in a cottage we dream of a palace" (63). Bachelard continues, "The two extreme realities of cottage and manor . . . take into account our need for retreat and expansion, for simplicity and magnificence" (65). Consequently, "the dream house must possess every virtue. However spacious, it must also be a cottage, a dovecote, a nest, a chrysalis. Intimacy needs the heart of a nest" (ibid.). The dimension of exile, however, is a variance that Bachelard's theory does not encompass, since for the narrator, Alicia, neither are apartments in Paris protective and welcoming nor are castles in the French countryside expansive and inspiring. Alicia's status both as the descendant of immigrants in Argentina and as an exile in France makes it difficult for her to establish a lasting home in the present.

As scholar Susanna Bachmann concludes in her analysis of *El árbol de la gitana*, Alicia's "multiple frustrated attempts in search of a fixed domicile in France" and ultimately "[t]he impossibility of installing herself definitively in an apartment" (79) constitute the main theme of Dujovne Ortiz's novel. In her dissertation, Carolina Rocha further observes that *El árbol de la gitana* "showcase[s] the loss or abandonment of an ideal house from the past, and this is a central metaphor of a ruptured nation, of a forfeited homeland" and refers to how "the rootlessness caused by migration is dramatized by the numerous descriptions of the houses that the narrator attempts to live in and finally abandons" (225). In similar terms, in his insightful article on Dujovne Ortiz, D. Jan Mennell discusses how "one can clearly see the sense of alienation that Alicia experiences in the different domiciles that she occupies throughout the text. She projects on the diverse dwellings belonging to others a series of violent emotions of rejection and active hostility" (9). In the sections of the novel that take place in France, the tenuousness of the protagonist's position is underscored by the fact that we find her house sitting for a friend, dwelling in decrepit castles in the French countryside, and renting an apartment in a condemned neighborhood in Paris. The description of her precarious residences, where her plastic suitcases imitate leather and the plastic furniture is embossed to simulate wood grain, highlight the narrator's perception of the transitory nature of her stay in France.

Furniture is a topic of contemplation throughout *El árbol de la gitana*. Like the space of the house itself, for Bachelard, "Wardrobes with their shelves, desks with their drawers, and chests with their false bottoms are veritable organs of the secret psychological life" (78). As anthropologist Mary Douglas observes, the imposition of order on space through the selection and arranging of furniture is a critical dimension of the definition of home (263). Because of this, furniture can have particular symbolic meaning for exiles. In the sardonic voice of Salman Rushdie's narrator in *The Satanic Verses*, "In exile, the furniture is ugly, expensive, all bought at the same time in the same store and in too much of a hurry" (214). The very thought of purchasing a piece of furniture that cannot be disassembled at a moment's notice represents a terrifying prospect for Alicia, as it connotes a sense of permanence that in her state of indefinite exile is alien to her. In her dissertation, Kelly Jensen specifically discusses Alicia's reluctance to purchase more durable furniture as a manifestation of her fear of establishing a home only to lose it again (228, 233).

The image of living indefinitely with temporary furniture or out of a suitcase is often used by those who write on the topic of exile. Dujovne Ortiz herself speaks of immigrants who spend "years without opening one's suitcase, in one's head or heart or in reality: I have known cases of immigrants who never worked up the nerve to unpack their things to put them in the wardrobe in their host countries" (*Al que se va* 36). As Vásquez and Araujo observe, "In the beginning, exiles are ashamed to settle in comfortably, they sleep on the floor, they have no furniture or dishes. They suppose they will only be away from their country for a short while" (47). Vásquez and Araujo explain that this sense of temporariness has an effect on human relations: "Since one is just passing through, one becomes easily installed in a provisional mode, with little or no furniture, one accepts any job, one establishes personal and social relations with the idea that they also are temporary" (33). As scholar Mary McCarthy asserts regarding exiles, "The whole point about them is their refusal to put down new roots . . . Even when they have funds to buy a little house, take a long lease on a flat, they prefer transient accommodations, bed-sitters or hotel rooms . . . If an exile buys a house or takes a long lease on a flat, it's a sign that he's no longer a true exile" (51). In *The Satanic Verses*, Rushdie's narrator concludes, "In exile all attempts to put down roots look like treason: they are admissions of defeat" (215). Since being an exile is an important facet of Alicia's identity, she is reluctant to settle into any one place in France.

As literary critics have observed, Dujovne Ortiz's autobiographical novel is structured as a dialectic between two absent ancestral homes (Mennell 3, 7; Jensen 221–22; Bachmann 82; Rocha 181). The very first words of *El árbol de la gitana* refer to Alicia's father's imagined ideal home: "Fata Morgana. This was the name of the house my father always wanted to have, the house of a child's drawing" (15). She goes on to describe a zigzagging pathway leading to a brick house with a gabled roof and smoke curling from the chimney toward the clouds, then clarifies that this perfect home is just a utopian dream, since her father never lived in such a house. The illusiveness of this image of home is underscored by the expression "Fata Morgana," which refers to a mirage. The second paragraph of the novel explains that, in contrast to her father's experience as the son of immigrants, her mother was "more Argentine" (ibid.) and thus her house was not a product of dreams for the future, but rather of memory of the past. Her mother's real but now lost home is described as having a balcony with a trellis, patios with roses and magnolias, and a bronze knocker on a solid wood door—that is, images of a childhood featuring the sense of intimacy, security, and permanence that home represents in Bachelard's philosophy.

But Alicia never lived in her mother's childhood home, and consequently only has access to it through the reconstruction of memory. The detailed tour that the narrator's description offers of this home she never knew, with all its rooms and patios, is reminiscent of *The Poetics of Space*: "[I]f the house is a bit elaborate, if it has a cellar and a garret, nooks and corridors, our memories have refuges that are all the more clearly delineated" (Bachelard 8). Her description of her mother's house also serves as an example of what scholar Marianne Hirsch would call "postmemory," which "characterizes the experience of those who grow up dominated by narratives that preceded their birth, whose own belated stories are displaced by the stories of the previous generation" (420). As the narrative proceeds, it becomes evident that her father's dream and her mother's memory are so powerful that they nearly overshadow Alicia's own experience of home.

The narrator observes that the legacy she inherits from her parents consists of these two absent homes, one imagined and the other remembered, as well as a more material but equally impermanent home, the apartment in Buenos Aires with a small patio containing overgrown geraniums where Alicia spent her own childhood. The transience of this domicile as well is underscored in *El árbol de la gitana*, since during the course of the novel the Buenos Aires apartment is sold following the death of Alicia's mother. The psychological impact of these lost and imagined homes leads the narrator to wonder how real estate anchored in the past and future can weigh so heavily upon the transplanted soul (16).

The narrator's house of memory, then, is created in the space between nostalgic longing for the past and anticipatory yearning for the future:

> One thinks one is living scattered among different houses, but that's not true. By being dreamed, houses allow themselves to be transformed into one single house, the little patio of overgrown geraniums of the Buenos Aires apartment flows into my mother's big, rambling house that I never knew, and into the Fata Morgana that ·my father imagined on Sunday strolls . . . when he would suddenly stop in front of a house with a garden, path, chimney and even the smoke curling up toward the clouds, and ask us anxiously, as if we were going to make an offer on the house the next day, "Do you like this one, girls?" (20)

The influence of Bachelard on this consolidated image of home is apparent, since he describes the space of home as fundamentally a space of dreams and memories: "Through dreams, the various dwelling-places in our lives co-penetrate and retain the treasure of former days . . . [T]he house is one of the greatest powers of integration for the thoughts, memories and dreams of mankind" (6). The image of packing suitcases is intimately related to the question of the preservation of memory. When Alicia is preparing to leave Argentina as a political exile, she compares the act of packing her bags to the process of writing: "[T]he basic problem was the baggage. The immigrant packs what is essential, and in defining what is essential, sets the tone for the future story. Just like a novelist when writing the first lines. But the brand-new brown imitation leather suitcases . . . looked at us perplexed. *They couldn't come up with the first line*" (17, emphasis mine). The choice of what to take into exile is perceived here as a transcendental decision that entails determining which elements of the past are going to accompany her into the future, as the narrator debates: "Will the suitcases hold my school notebooks and my daughter's, that is, memory, or things that are important for today?" (17). Alicia's impulse is to prioritize nostalgia for the past over present necessities, a factor that will frustrate future attempts to form a home in France, as she continues to employ memory as the material from which to build her own "Fata Morgana."

Prior to the protagonist's exile, her mother, who had remained in Argentina, urged her to take warm clothes for the European winter. Alicia had foolishly believed that if she left them in France they would be waiting for her when she returned: "With a shiver that we later understood, my mother insisted on adding to our immigrant trousseau wool hats, socks and scarves, that, after a heated discussion, returned to the wardrobe that has now disappeared and become the object of troubled reflection. Where is that wardrobe now, the one from my childhood? Who has taken it away in spite of its wood grain that looked like faces on feverish nights?" (17–18).

The sense of grief is patent here, as the disappearance of the wardrobe symbolizes the exile's loss of home and family. But neither the wardrobe nor Alicia's childhood home will ever be recuperated, since after her mother's death, to pay her rent in Paris, she sells the Buenos Aires apartment.

The narrator draws on the image of the lost wardrobe to reflect on the state of exile overall: "The mistake was thinking, it doesn't matter, these knitted socks can stay at home, in this same drawer where

I will find them waiting for me when I return . . . The mistake was thinking that the exile returns. That one's house is waiting for one. And that one's mother is still there knitting" (18). Bachelard's words address the importance of memory in the face of loss: "[T]he houses that were lost forever continue to live on in us" (56). Although she is far away, the Buenos Aires apartment, where Alicia used to dress up as a gypsy and daydream, lives on in the narrator's memory. This corresponds to Bachelard's assertion that "[t]he house we were born in is more than an embodiment of home, it is also an embodiment of dreams. Each one of its nooks and corners was a resting-place for daydreaming" (15).

Upon arriving in France, Alicia attempts to settle into "Meudon, noble Parisian neighborhood with noble stone façades where I ended up with my thirteen-year-old daughter and the two brown imitation leather suitcases" (51). The narrator observes that in spite of the charming tile roofs, gardens, and curling smoke, life in exile is isolating; and this neighborhood does not provide her and her daughter with the warmth and intimacy of home.

The apartment in Meudon is the first of many French homes that greet Alicia with hostility rather than comfort: "Far away, at our feet, Paris. I would have been happy with a view that was less majestuous but more comforting. The silence was alive. Upon returning home, the lock to the main door was frozen. It was hard to get the key in, and in order to get into the two-room furnished apartment, we had to jump over the debris in the front yard . . . abandoned baby carriages, old mattresses, and rusted water heaters exposed to the elements" (52).

Alicia realizes that she is in no position to reproach her landlady about the debris in the front yard, since she herself as an exile is carrying around suitcases filled with the rubble of her past. Since, for Bachelard, "A lock is a psychological threshold" (82–84), here, the obstacles in the yard, the silence, and most poignantly the frozen lock can be seen as images representing the narrator's lack of a sense of belonging in France.

From Meudon, Alicia moves to an apartment in Gaité, which she believes will be more welcoming, but Gaité turns out to be a condemned neighborhood whose original occupants have gradually been displaced by immigrants from the third world. The few remaining French belong to the "fourth world" of extreme poverty. In this immigrant quarter, the narrator again feels that she is surrounded by rubble that is beginning to suffocate her. Her sense of not belonging is heightened by the nocturnal singing of a neighbor lady who bellows out "Je ne suis pas d'ici" ("I am not from here" 54), reminding the narrator of her own precarious position as exile, as she strains not to cry out in response, "Neither am I" (ibid.).

In spite of the fact that demolition has already begun in the condemned neighborhood, Alicia remains in Gaité and fills her apartment with the cast-off furniture that a neighbor was storing among sundry surplus items heaped in the basement. The narrator interprets these items as the raw materials for a narrative, but she is unfamiliar with their history. Thus she takes a metal cupboard, apparently intended as a china cabinet, and "translates" it as a file cabinet to safeguard the papers about her ancestors that form the basis of her family tree narrated in alternate chapters of *El árbol de la gitana*. Within her logic, the choice of a kitchen cupboard for her papers makes sense, since throughout the novel the narrator repeatedly reminds the reader that she does not know how to cook, only how to write.

With this borrowed furniture, she settles into the condemned neighborhood, but once again the warmth and intimacy of home eludes her. Her description of opening the metal cabinet reminds one of a haunted house: "I opened the cabinet. I put my hand in. The gale that was blowing through the corridors of the towers, upset by the bulldozer, seemed to have sunk into the lower shelf, where the brown portfolio tied with hairy twine with the story of my ancestors laid dormant" (60). With this, the protagonist begins to compose the narrative of her family history from the papers stored in the reinterpreted china cabinet, signaling how the nurturing center of the house of memory that she is building to fill the cold, forbidding places of her exile is not the kitchen, but the writing desk.

Confronted with writer's block, Alicia goes to a friend's country house in L'Ile de France for inspiration, carrying her imitation leather suitcase with the brown portfolio tied with the hairy twine. Like in the city, in the countryside, houses refuse to open their arms to her. Her friend's country manor is portrayed as animal-like in that it manifests its distrust of strangers by baring its teeth and growling at her when she tries to insert the key in the lock. The furniture appears hostile as well, in particular a chest of drawers carved with a depiction of hares eating pears and pears eating hares. When, after a night of insomnia, she ventures into the garden, Alicia is attacked by a grapevine that tries to suck the juices out of her. She retreats to the wine cellar but fearing another assault, she ends up going into the study and sitting down at her desk. If nothing else, the experience seems to have cured her of writing block, since she begins to write the history of her "blood," defying the vampire-like furniture that threatens to suck her dry. This image of devouring will follow Alicia through her various country abodes throughout the novel.

Following the scene at the country manor, the protagonist's daughter, now 17 years old, declares that she is going to leave France for the Amazon in order to look for her roots, even though she is descended from European immigrants to Argentina, not indigenous peoples of the Amazon. Alicia regrets that neither their native country nor the host country she has chosen for them can provide her daughter with the sense of rootedness for which she longs. The narrator wishes she could be more like a geranium that could grow in just a little bit of earth in the patio of her family's Buenos Aires apartment, since if exile had not been her fate, then her daughter would not be wandering around the jungle looking for her roots.

After her daughter leaves for South America, the demolition of the condemned neighborhood of Gaité continues, and as a result Alicia begins to live in a series of castles. The first one, in La Nièvre, belongs to a friend who offers it to her as a place to think. Her friend's castle has a tower in ruins in which animals make noises that give the impression of a haunted house. This makes it an ideal environment for the narrator to contemplate and write about her "real and imagined ancestors" (109). Alicia experiences a ghost entering her body and feels that the castle is eager to devour her. This leads her to meditate on her relationship with her various dwellings: "I happen to be here by pure coincidence, without any of the houses or castles that I stumble across being either my mother's lost home or my father's Fata Morgana. Neither do I recognize them nor do I awaken remembrance in them. What I awaken in them is their appetite. A house or castle that sees me in these parts starts to lick its chops . . .

How strange, Europe, all this broken stone with an age-old hunger" (ibid.).

The very next day Alicia hastily grabs her papers and escapes to Paris. After the hungry castle, the condemned Gaité seems like a safe nest. Although her building is a historical monument, it is also scheduled for demolition since it is so dilapidated that it is beginning to collapse. Before abandoning her apartment to live at the religious retreat of the Château de Chichy, she sorts through her belongings to decide which items she can part with and which will accompany her in her future wanderings. As when she had left Argentina for exile, a piece of furniture is featured as center stage in this deliberation; in this case it is her daughter's wooden wardrobe, which had replaced a plastic wardrobe embossed with imitation wood grain that had previously stood as an emblem of the tentativeness of their situation of exile.

The narrator recalls the day that she and her daughter bought the wooden wardrobe, and the sense of permanence this purchase had inspired in both mother and daughter: "Buying the real wooden wardrobe had represented a social advance. My daughter and I had gone into the furniture store with a dignified and elegant air, conscious that the acquisition of a wardrobe is a constructive moment that demonstrates one's solidity . . . After buying the wardrobe, how secure we felt, how stable was our life" (143–44). When Alicia puts her hand inside it in order to sort through her teenager's belongings, the wardrobe reacts by attempting to strangle her. This leads her to inquire, "What am I supposed to do? Should I keep my daughter's pajamas from when she was seven years old, or should I let go altogether, as free as the wind?" (144). Ultimately, she selects certain representative items, resulting in "baggage prepared with subtle balance, as if I had used a scale for weighing pearls—a few grams of childhood here, an ounce of adolescence there—the suitcase was ready, and the wardrobe was reduced to bare boards" (144).

Alicia gives away most of her daughter's clothing to the residents of the Château de Chichy, where she reassembles the wooden wardrobe. When her friend Mireille arrives for a visit and discerns the unsuitability of her living arrangement, she whisks Alicia back to Paris, forcing her to leave behind the wardrobe, which does not fit in Mireille's car. The one possession that remains with the protagonist throughout her journey is the brown portfolio tied with hairy twine containing the stories of her ancestors, her only link to the past. As the narrator observes, "Without that portfolio, I would be pure future" (149).

Back in Paris, Alicia housesits for her friend while she is away on vacation. Because Mireille's apartment constitutes another temporary home, she is hesitant to settle in. After dwelling in places that snarled at her, expelled her, or attempted to devour her, Mireille's apartment, in turn, sniffs and licks her like a dog. Alicia tries to settle down into an overstuffed chair, reveling in its solidity, even though in her precarious situation as housesitter, she knows she cannot get too comfortable: "The easy chair was as generous as a port. When I sat in it, I felt as if I had arrived. It didn't escape me that my position in it was fragile, though" (179). As a wanderer, she has learned not to be overconfident in the protective nature of inviting furniture. When the easy chair, which evidently has a history of being the site of amorous trysts, tries to get too intimate with her, she opts instead for an austere chair, after enjoying "a mere instant of the pure privilege of living, in an overstuffed chair in a borrowed house" (ibid.). She nevertheless longs for the sensation that "a traveler who has frequently packed and unpacked bags with tears in his eyes experiences before an immense creature all made of velvet, with both arms reaching out toward him saying, 'Come, don't worry'" (ibid.). Like the intimacy of home, the familiarity of furniture is something that the narrator feels she is barred from both as an exile and as the daughter of generations of immigrants.

Eventually she begins to feel more at ease, and curiosity leads her to peer inside every closed container in Mireille's apartment. For Bachelard, the idea that boxes are associated with intimacy is self-evident: "[C]hests and caskets . . . are very evident witnesses of the *need for secrecy*, of an intuitive sense of hiding places. It is not merely a matter of keeping a possession well-guarded . . . [T]he fact that there should exist a homology between the geometry of the small box and the psychology of secrecy does not call for protracted comment" (81–82). Snooping in every nook and cranny, the narrator uncovers her friend's secrets: "Unable to help myself, I got up from the motherly easy chair and began the task of opening up Mireille's house one lid at a time, like pulling the petals off the daisy of being her" (180).

Upon opening up her wardrobe, Alicia reveals the history of all the women in Mireille's family. As Bachelard remarks, "Every poet of furniture . . . knows that the inner space of an old wardrobe is deep. A wardrobe's inner space is also *intimate space*, space that is not open to just anybody" (78). Although this wardrobe also threatens to strangle her, the narrator is enticed to wear her friend's clothes and take over her identity, to the extent that she spends the night with one of Mireille's lovers. Since she is housesitting, however, this situation is temporary and Alicia soon goes back to her own apartment and her own life.

While visiting her daughter in Colombia, the narrator finds out that her mother has died. The sale of the Buenos Aires apartment provides Alicia with the means to sign a lease rather than subletting. Although she has rented a new apartment in Paris, once again she is drawn to castles, this time one in the Loire Valley. While walking her dog, Alicia tells the canine that even gypsies eventually yearn to settle down, and declares that she will remain in this small town until she dies, but even the dog knows her well enough to say with his eyes, "I don't think you will stay here or anywhere" (215). In the Loire Valley, Alicia is unable to find a country house that meets her father's criteria of Fata Morgana, so she once again heads back to Paris.

Her stay in Paris is short lived, however. After having spent all the money from the sale of her mother's home, or in the narrator's words, having "eaten all the bricks from the apartment in Buenos Aires" (219), Alicia has a new reason to wish to build a nest—her daughter is expecting a child to "repopulate the family" (ibid.). Alicia applies for a grant. While awaiting the results she decides to sublet her Parisian apartment and housesit. Once again, she ends up in a cold and musty castle, this time in a remote northern province.

At the castle in Grampcel, Alicia ventures into the cellar, but she finds it to be forbidding and seeks instead the comfort and refuge of her bed, "like a geranium in a small pot that they suddenly transplanted into a huge pot full of fresh soil" (230). As an exile and as the descendant of immigrants, Alicia clearly has difficulty finding a Bachelardian balance between the cozy cottage and the spacious palace. As she observes, "I am full of ruins, my own and those of others" (231).

It is also while she is in Grampcel that the gypsy woman remarks that since the Dirty War is over in Argentina, there is nothing stopping Alicia from returning home. The narrator knows that the usual clichés such as "foreignness is a country" and "one must be far from one's country to understand it better" are not adequate to express her decision to remain abroad, and so she candidly remarks, "The dictatorship ended in Argentina but not inside me" (225). Upon arriving at the castle, the narrator had observed that by this time her imitation leather suitcases had lost their handles, signaling that the transitory nature of the exile's lifestyle is beginning to wear thin. The notion that she needs to buy either new luggage or more permanent furniture symbolizes Alicia's recognition that she faces a choice between returning to Argentina and remaining in France.

After the birth of her granddaughter and the award of a grant to write her family history, Alicia once again moves back to Paris, where the issue of furniture reemerges: "I seemed settled, but the objects around me were still roaming" (232). Having returned borrowed furniture to its owners, Alicia contemplates purchasing a solid easy chair, but she ends up retreating from such an ominous commitment: "I had decided to buy an imposing chair, one that can't be taken apart, like the one Mireille has, with a roll of velvet to support the neck and two protective arms reaching out to me. It wasn't because of the price that I left the furniture store with a miniscule folding chair under my arm. It was the voice inside me that whispered, 'If you move again, what will you do with a chair that size?'" (232). Once again, Alicia realizes that as an exile such a sense of permanence is categorically forbidden to her.

When her grant comes to its end, her daughter and granddaughter return to Colombia with the imitation leather suitcases, and Alicia soon follows sporting brand new luggage. Upon arriving in Bogotá, she observes that the name of the airport, El Dorado, suggests the kind of paradise that leads her to believe that she may find her father's idyllic homestead there. The idea that it is family that truly constitutes home is evoked when the narrator says, "The feeling of having arrived became a certainty when I embraced all three: my daughter, my granddaughter and her father" (283). Although both El Dorado and Fata Morgana suggest illusions, her daughter's colonial-style abode does to a certain extent resemble her composite ideal of home, in that it has a trellised balcony, a bronze knocker on a solid wood door, and a patio filled with the familiar roses and magnolias, as well as tropical flowers with which she is unfamiliar. After conducting a Bachelardian reconnaissance of the space, the narrator reaches an ambiguous conclusion: "It was the house of memory and it was not, because history never repeats itself in exactly the same way" (284).

Curiously, after describing her daughter's uncannily familiar home in Bogotá, the narrator flashes back to an earlier trip to Argentina prior to her mother's death: "So complete was the illusion of having arrived, and of living in the house of memory, that I took a break, and remembered my mother's face" (284). Following the fall of the dictatorship, Alicia had spent two months with her mother in the Buenos Aires apartment where she grew up, and during this time, she experienced failed attempts to visit some former residences. Notably, she discovered that the house where she and her mother had lived when her father was a political prisoner in the 1940s had been replaced by skyscrapers. She also visited a purely vertical house with each room on a different level; although it was never her home, this place exercises considerable force in Alicia's memory, since she had wanted to live there but her erstwhile partner had preferred a solid house on a ground floor. She attributes the dissolution of that relationship in part to this discrepancy between domestic visions. While visiting this "dwelling where I attempted to live and whose very impossibility had transformed it into memory" (286), she receives a threatening glance from a resident and feels that she is once again being expelled. The fact that she is narrating this to us after having found her daughter's home in Bogotá that so closely approximates her house of memory indicates that even with this positive experience she cannot transcend her ingrained association of home with loss and impermanence.

In her interview with Leonardo Senkman, Dujovne Ortiz reveals that originally her daughter's home was going to form the ending of the novel: "My daughter decides to look for her roots in Latin America. She traveled a lot, she married a Colombian, she has a daughter; the novel was going to end in El Dorado, and since it is a search for paradises, it was going to end with a big colonial house in Bogotá, where the family is" (Senkman 92). Dujovne Ortiz resists this facile conclusion, however, opting instead to leave her protagonist in a perpetual state of exile without having settled permanently in the longed-for home. Still feeling the sense of well-being that the family visit inspires in her, Alicia returns to France with the intent of making an itinerant home by traveling back and forth between Paris and Bogotá, in a manner reminiscent of what Trinh Minh-ha describes when she says in reference to exiles who choose this lifestyle, "Thus, figuratively but also literally speaking, traveling back and forth between home and abroad becomes a mode of dwelling" (14–15). Alicia is never able to put her plan of an itinerant home into action, however, since her daughter announces that her Bogotá home also must return to the space of memory and dreams, presumably because of Colombia's increase in violence in general and in particular toward Jews in the late 1980s. The novel ends with Alicia attending a conference in Israel on Jewish writers in exile after inviting her daughter to join her in Paris.

In her interview with Senkman, which took place in Israel while she was still finishing her autobiographical novel, Dujovne Ortiz describes *El árbol de la gitana* in her own words: "[W]hat unites these characters is me, exiled in Paris, with the folder with dad's diary, trying to write this novel and living in crazy places, in servants' quarters, in castles, in houses, in cottages, and all the time being a woman struggling with the most concrete aspects of daily life, for survival and the obsession with writing an impossible novel, as I am impossible, a series of fragments" (Senkman 91).

For Bachelard, "With the house image we are in possession of a veritable principle of psychological integration" (xxxii). But as we have seen, for Dujovne Ortiz, a permanent home—and the psychological integration it represents—are perceived as out of reach.

Much has been written in recent years on the topic of how the very idea of "home" needs to be critically reevaluated in our mobile world, in this age of globalization. As Mennell observes, by the end of *El árbol de la gitana*, the narrator becomes aware of the "unachievable nature of her homeless migration. The home she seeks cannot exist anywhere, since her notion of home is a work in progress, not a definitive and concrete reality" (10). This assertion harks back to the passage from Bachelard that Dujovne Ortiz's narrator quotes on one of her many train trips back to Paris: "Maybe it is a good thing for us to keep a few dreams of a house that we shall live in later, always later, so much later, in fact, that we shall not have time to achieve it. For a house that was final, one that stood in symmetrical relation to the house we were born in, would lead to thoughts—serious, sad thoughts—and not to dreams. It is better to live in a state of impermanence than in one of finality" (Bachelard 61; Dujovne Ortiz 218). As Edward Said observes along similar lines, "The exile knows that in a secular and contingent world, homes are always provisional" (365). Dujovne Ortiz's novel is a tale of loss and recuperation, but in Bachelard's words, "we must lose our earthly Paradise in order actually to live in it" (33). In *Buenos Aires*, Dujovne Ortiz refers to Argentines in general as having a sense of belonging only to a lost paradise (43).

Near the end of the novel, the ghosts of her ancestors tell Alicia that in the face of centuries of loss, what she is looking for she will find inside herself. The gypsy woman—who at first seems to be Alicia herself and in the end appears as her mother—represents a positive valorization of the wandering that is inevitable in the narrator's state of exile. The gypsy woman laughs in the face of Alicia's desire for stability: "She gave me the present of the tree of stories. She also pushed me from move to move. My craving for real estate is foreign to her. She doesn't find the thread of sense under a roof. She knows that my house of gables is a book. But she makes fun of my idea of a permanent home. 'You are stubborn,' she tells me, watching me try to drag my four walls of truth around the world" (24).

Regarding the family history Alicia is writing, the gypsy woman says, "Think of each page as a brick of the home of your birth" (215). Thus the answer is that her legacy is not to be found in the physical space of four walls, but in the tales of her ancestors, which the gypsy woman helps her weave into a portable "house of memory."

Works Cited

Alegría, Fernando. "One True Sentence." Trans. Kathleen McNerny. *Altogether Elsewhere: Writers on Exile*. Ed. Marc Robinson. Boston: Faber and Faber, 1994. 193–98. Print.

Bachelard, Gaston. *The Poetics of Space*. Trans. Maria Jolas. Boston: Beacon, 1969. Print.

Bachmann, Susanna. *Topografías del doble lugar: El exilio literario visto por nueve autoras del cono sur*. Saragossa: Pórtico, 2002. Print.

Bammer, Angelika. "Introduction." *Displacements: Cultural Identities in Question*. Ed. Angelika Bammer. Bloomington: Indiana UP, 1994. xi-xx. Print.

Benedetti, Mario. *Andamios*. Buenos Aires: Seix Barral, 1996. Print.

———. *El desexilio y otras conjeturas*. Buenos Aires: Nueva Imagen, 1985. Print.

———. *Primavera con una esquina rota*. Mexico City: Nueva Imagen, 1982. Print.

Borinsky, Alicia. "Gombrowicz's Tango: An Argentine Snapshot." *Exile and Creativity: Signposts, Travelers, Outsiders, Backward Glances*. Durham: Duke UP, 1998. 143–62. Print.

Brah, Avtar. *Cartographies of Diaspora: Contesting Identities*. London: Routledge, 1996. Print.

Breytenbach, Breyten. "A Letter from Exile, to Don Espejuelo." *Altogether Elsewhere: Writers on Exile*. Ed. Marc Robinson. Boston: Faber and Faber, 1994. 12–16. Print.

Bryce Echenique, Alfredo. *Crónicas personales*. Barcelona: Anagrama, 1988. Print.

Burke, Peter. "History as Social Memory." *Memory: History, Culture and the Mind*. Ed. Thomas Butler. Oxford: Blackwell, 1989. 97–113. Print.

Carter, Erica, James Donald, and Judith Squires, eds. *Space and Place: Theories of Identity and Location*. London: Lawrence and Wishart, 1993. Print.

Chambers, Iain. *Migrancy, Culture, Identity*. New York: Routledge, 1994. Print.

Cortázar, Julio. "The Fellowship of Exile." Trans. John Incledon. *Altogether Elsewhere: Writers on Exile*. Ed. Marc Robinson. Boston: Faber and Faber, 1994. 171–78. Print.

Del Olmo, Margarita. *La utopía en el exilio*. Madrid: Consejo Superior de Investigaciones Científicas, 2002. Print.

Douglas, Mary. "The Idea of a Home: A Kind of Space." *Home: A Place in the World*. Ed. Arien Mack. New York: New York UP, 1993. 261–81. Print.

Dujovne Ortiz, Alicia. *Al que se va*. Buenos Aires: Zorzal, 2002. Print.

———. *El árbol de la gitana*. 1991. Trans. Alicia Dujovne Ortiz. Buenos Aires: Alfaguara, 1997. Print.

———. *Buenos Aires*. Paris: Champ Vallon, 1984. Print.

———. *María Elena Walsh*. 1979. Madrid: Júcar, 1982. Print.

Fernández Baraibar, Julio. "Volver, sea pato o gallareta." *La Argentina exiliada*. Ed. Daniel Parcero, Marcelo Helfgot, and Diego Dulce. Buenos Aires: Centro Editor de América Latina, 1985. 45–51. Print.

Fey, Ingrid E. "Frou-Frous or Feminists? Turn-of-the-Century Paris and the Latin American Woman." *Strange Pilgrimages: Exile, Travel, and National Identity in Latin America, 1800–1990s*. Ed. Ingrid E. Fey and Karen Racine. Wilmington: Scholarly Resources, 2000. 81–94. Print.

Fey, Ingrid E., and Karen Racine. "Introduction: National Identity Formation in an International Context." *Strange Pilgrimages: Exile, Travel, and National Identity in Latin America, 1800–1990s*. Ed. Ingrid E. Fey and Karen Racine. Wilmington: Scholarly Resources, 2000. xi–xix. Print.

Foster, David William. "Los parámetros de la narrativa argentina durante el 'Proceso de Reorganización Nacional.'" *Ficción y política: La narrativa argentina durante el proceso militar*. Buenos Aires: Alianza; Minneapolis: Institute for the Study of Ideologies and Literature, 1987. 96–108. Print.

Franco, Marina, and Pilar González Bernaldo. "Cuando el sujeto deviene objeto: La construcción del exilio argentino en Francia." *Represión y destierro: Itinerarios del exilio argentino*. Comp. Pablo Yankelevich. Buenos Aires: Ediciones al Margen, 2004. 17–47. Print.

Gasquet, Axel. "Prólogo." *La literatura expatriada: Conversaciones con escritores argentinos en París*. Santa Fe, Argentina: Universidad Nacional del Litoral, 2004. 7–10. Print.

Gass, William. "Exile." *Altogether Elsewhere: Writers on Exile*. Ed. Marc Robinson. Boston: Faber and Faber, 1994. 211–28. Print.

Guelar, Diana, Vera Jarach, and Beatriz Ruiz, eds. *Los chicos del exilio: Argentina (1975–1984)*. Buenos Aires: El País de Nomeolvides, 2002. Print.

Gurr, Andrew. *Writers in Exile: The Identity of Home in Modern Literature*. Sussex: Harvester/Atlantic; Highlands, New Jersey: Humanities, 1981. Print.

Hirsch, Marianne. "Past Lives: Postmemories in Exile." *Exile and Creativity: Signposts, Travelers, Outsiders, Backward Glances*. Ed. Susan Rubin Suleiman. Durham: Duke UP, 1998. 418–46. Print.

Jensen, Kelly Cathleen. "Un estudio del hogar diaspórico mediante novelas de seis escritoras exiliadas: Isabel Allende, Alicia Dujovne Ortiz, Luisa Futoransky, Sara Gallardo, Marta Traba y Ana Vasquez." Diss. U of Georgia, 2000.

Jones, Julie. *A Common Place: The Representation of Paris in Spanish American Fiction*. Lewisburg: Bucknell UP; London: Associated UPs, 1998. Print.

Kaminsky, Amy. *After Exile: Writing the Latin American Diaspora*. Minneapolis: U of Minneapolis P, 1999. Print.

Kennedy, J. Gerald. *Imagining Paris: Exile, Writing, and American Identity.* New Haven: Yale UP, 1993. Print.

Kramer, Lloyd S. *Threshold of a New World: Intellectuals and the Exile Experience in Paris, 1830–48.* Ithaca: Cornell UP, 1988. Print.

Mack, Arien, ed. *Home: A Place in the World.* New York: New York UP, 1993. Print.

McCarthy, Mary. "A Guide to Exiles, Expatriates, and Internal Émigrés." *Altogether Elsewhere: Writers on Exile.* Ed. Marc Robinson. Boston: Faber and Faber, 1994. 49–58. Print.

Mennell, D. Jan. "Entre el patio añorado y el patio anhelado: Una judía argentina errante en *El árbol de la gitana* de Alicia Dujovne Ortiz." *Lucero* 10 (1999): 3–11. Print.

Minh-ha, Trinh T. "Other than Myself/My Other Self." *Travellers' Tales: Narratives of Home and Displacement.* Ed George Robertson et al. London: Routledge, 1994. 9–26. Print.

Moraña, Mabel. "(Im)pertinencia de la memoria histórica en América Latina." *Memoria colectiva y políticas de olvido. Argentina y Uruguay, 1970–1990.* Ed. Adriana J. Bergero and Fernando Reati. Rosario, Argentina: Beatriz Viterbo, 1997. 31–41. Print.

Nouzeilles, Gabriela, and Graciela Montaldo. "General Introduction." *The Argentina Reader: History, Culture, Politics.* Eds. Gabriela Nouzeilles and Graciela Montaldo. Durham: Duke UP, 2002. 1–14. Print.

Perelli, Carina. "Memoria de Sangre: Fear, Hope, and Disenchantment in Argentina." *Remapping Memory: The Politics of TimeSpace.* Ed. Jonathan Boyarin. Minneapolis: U of Minnesota P, 1994. 39–66. Print.

Rapport, Nigel, and Andrew Dawson, eds. "Home and Movement: A Polemic." *Migrants of Identity: Perceptions of Home in a World of Movement.* New York: Oxford, 1998. Print.

Reati, Fernando. "Introduction." *Memoria colectiva y políticas de olvido. Argentina y Uruguay, 1970–1990.* Ed. Adriana J. Bergero and Fernando Reati. Rosario, Argentina: Beatriz Viterbo, 1997. 11–28. Print.

Renan, Ernest. "What Is a Nation?" 1882. Trans. Martin Thom. *Nation and Narration.* Ed. Homi Bhabha. London: Routledge, 1990. 8–22. Print.

Robertson, George, et al., eds. *Travellers' Tales: Narratives of Home and Displacement.* London: Routledge, 1994. 1–6. Print.

Robinson, Marc. "Introduction." *Altogether Elsewhere: Writers on Exile.* Ed. Marc Robinson. Boston: Faber and Faber, 1994. xi–xxii. Print.

Rocha, Carolina M. "Writing Memory or Memory Writing: *Santo oficio de la memoria, La madriguera, El árbol de la gitana.*" Diss. U Texas Austin, 2001.

Rushdie, Salman. *Imaginary Homelands: Essays and Criticism 1981–1991.* London: Granta, 1991. Print.

————. *The Satanic Verses. A Novel*. New York: Holt, 1988. Print.

————. *Shame*. New York: Knopf, 1983. Print.

Said, Edward. "Reflections on Exile." *Out There: Marginalization and Contemporary Cultures*. Ed. Russell Ferguson, Martha Gever, Trinh Minhha, and Cornel West. New York: New Museum of Contemporary Art; Cambridge: MIT P, 1991. 357–66. Print.

Sarlo, Beatriz. "El campo intelectual: Un espacio doblemente fracturado." *Represión y reconstrucción de una cultura: El caso argentino*. Comp. Saúl Sosnowski. Buenos Aires: Editorial Universitaria de Buenos Aires, 1988. 95–107. Print.

Schwartz, Marcy E. *Writing Paris: Urban Topographies of Desire in Contemporary Latin American Fiction*. Albany: State U of New York P, 1999. Print.

Senkman, Leonardo. "Entrevista a Alicia Dujovne Ortiz: Las tribulaciones de un centauro argentino exiliado en París." *Noaj* 1.2 (1988): 87–95. Print.

————. "La nación imaginaria de los escritores judíos latinoamericanos." *Revista Iberoamericana* 66.191 (2000): 279–98. Print.

Siedel, Michael. *Exile and the Narrative Imagination*. New Haven: Yale UP, 1986. Print.

Sosnowski, Saúl. "Políticas de la memoria y del olvido." *Memoria colectiva y políticas de olvido. Argentina y Uruguay, 1970–1990*. Ed. Adriana J. Bergero and Fernando Reati. Rosario, Argentina: Beatriz Viterbo, 1997. 43–58. Print.

————. "Introducción." *Represión y reconstrucción de una cultura: El caso argentino*. Comp. Saúl Sosnowski. Buenos Aires: Editorial Universitaria de Buenos Aires, 1988. 7–18. Print.

Spalek, John M. "The Varieties of Exile Experience: German, Polish, and Spanish Writers." *Latin America and the Literature of Exile*. Ed. Hans-Bernhard Moeller. Heidelberg: Carl Winter/Universitätsverlag, 1983. 71–90. Print.

Suleiman, Susan Rubin, ed. *Exile and Creativity: Signposts, Travelers, Outsiders, Backward Glances*. Ed. Susan Rubin Suleiman. Durham: Duke UP, 1998. 1–6. Print.

Tangos: El exilio de Gardel. Dir. Fernando E. Solanas, 1985. Print.

Taylor, Diana. *Disappearing Acts: Spectacles of Gender and Nationalism in Argentina's "Dirty War."* Durham: Duke UP, 1997. Print.

Timerman, Jacobo. *Prisoner without a Name, Cell without a Number*. Trans. Toby Talbot. New York: Knopf, 1981. Print.

Vásquez, Ana, and Ana María Araujo. *Exils latino-américains. La malédiction d'Ulysse*. Paris: CIEMI/Harmattan, 1988.

4

Writing from the Margins, Writing in the Margins

Christa Wolf's *Medea*

Adelheid Eubanks

Overview

*B*orn 1929 in Landsburg an der Warthe, Germany, today Polish Gorzow Wielkopolski, Christa Wolf has been one of the most influential figures in German literature since 1961. The reunification of the two Germanies in 1990 entailed a marginalization of Wolf and her fellow East German writers in that many of them felt they had been "exiled" or "colonized" by the West. During the Literaturstreit (literature battle), West German critics and intellectuals, in turn, debated the question whether or not East German writers could still be considered artists at a time when their point of reference, the East German state, no longer existed. In an attempt to deal with the many allegations and accusations against her work and her person, Wolf embarked on a voluntary and temporary "exile" in the United States, where much work was done on her first major "post-reunification" novel, Medea (1996; English translation 1998). The text features the author's usual writerly concerns involving relationships between past and present, men and women, individual and society, and so on in a retelling of Euripides's tragedy. Wolf presents a modern(ized) Medea who becomes comprehensible as woman, as victim, and as outsider. Wolf's Medea attains new meaning in the context *of political oppression in general and the former East German regime in particular. The ways in which Wolf chooses to modernize the protagonist point to a subtler level of the novel where one reads Wolf's text in the context of recent German history, the questions regarding identity and community since reunification, and more generally the history of Western civilization.*

Under the old *Grundgesetz* (basic constitutional law of West Germany), East and West Germany could unite in accordance with either article 23 or article 146. The latter article relates to the period of validity of the constitution and would have allowed all Germans to replace the existing constitution with a new one. The former article stipulated that the West German law be extended to apply to East Germany and its citizens. Since the October 3, 1990, unification proceeded in compliance with the provisions of article 23, the German Democratic Republic (GDR) ceased to exist and renowned author Christa Wolf and fellow East German citizens became exiles.

"Exile," Nico Israel writes, "tends to imply both a coherent subject . . . and a more circumscribed, limited conception of place and home" (3). On October 2, 1990, East Germans lived in a state that was based on socialist ideology and economy. The next day, the new frame of reference, by law, became democratic. East German subjects thus were displaced politically and ideologically.[1] Many East Germans have since felt this displacement and expressed this sense literally as feelings of loss and alienation. Both of these feelings, in turn, are often linked to questions of personal and national identity.[2]

The following sections of this chapter inquire into Christa Wolf's *Medea* and into what this work offers in the context of a reunified Germany. It is appropriate to situate both the novel and its author in a particular context. Therefore, first I briefly discuss the divergent histories of the two German states, with special emphasis on the concept of national identity. The historical section highlights the extend to which East Germans, as well as West Germans, today are still struggling to construct their place within the new Germany. In the second section, the historical background leads to Christa Wolf and an understanding of the author's particular situation, which I consider to be that of an exile. Third, I will read Wolf's *Medea* in terms of the novel's treatment of the concepts of exile and displacement. Lastly, I suggest that Wolf's *Medea* offers, both directly and indirectly, commentary on the ongoing quest for Germany's reunification and its pursuit of a postunification identity.

"Nation-ness, as well as nationalism, are cultural artefacts of a particular kind," notes Benedict Anderson (4). These artefacts, Benedict's "imagined communities," are important in that the concept of nation provides a sense of identity for an individual and "fulfills," in Stephen Barbour's words, "a need for a sense of community" ("Nationalism" 14). Barbour explains that the foundations of nations can be "territorial and regional, religious, as well as linguistic and administrative" (ibid. 13). Given these bases, Germany has had a problematic history with itself as nation. In terms of territory, it became a nation only in the 1870s. Moreover, after 1945, Germany became two distinct and separate German states. In addition, Germany was also never a nation bound by a common religion or a common language.[3] For at least two reasons, an already complex issue with regard to the German nation and a German identity became even more so after World War II. First, both East and West Germany still lacked the foundations that can aid in creating a nation (such as the common religion and language). Second, East and West Germany had to situate themselves against the Nazi regime. The two states did so in very different ways.

To summarize the postwar changes, East Germany created a completely new and socialist identity that relied on and stressed collective effort and demanded the citizens' loyalty to the *sozialistisches Vaterland*, the socialist fatherland. East Germans saw the end of World War II as the defeat of capitalism. Socialist and communist intellectuals in the German Democratic Republic (GDR) argued that East Germans were victims of both capitalism and the Nazi regime. While it is debatable to what degree East Germans identified with the state and its ideology, they nonetheless were part of a society that had its distinct cultural, social, ideological, and political profile. It seems natural that East Germans would develop questions of identity upon unification, for the reason that the state in which they had lived and worked no longer existed.[4]

The Federal Republic of Germany (FRG), on the other hand, was a democracy and defined itself in terms of capitalist values, technological and economic progress, and the individual's entrepreneurship. The FRG, instead of rejecting the Nazi past, engaged in what is commonly referred to as *Vergangenheitsbewältigung* (overcoming the past). Importantly, the shared past prevented the creation of an "imagined community," a collective identity, because this very past was and is fraught with horror and nothing but negative models. West Germans thus struggled with the concept of national identity and tended to favor regional and/or international—that is, European—options.[5]

Upon unification, then, the situation was an intricate one for *both* East and West Germans, and, as Sager notes, "individual and national identities experienced discontinuities" (277). Against the background of the constitution, it appears that West Germans had an advantage over East Germans. Indeed, many efforts aimed at devaluing the former East German regime as an "*Unrechts-Staat*, that is both unjust and unconstitutional" (Weedon 224). The implication is that the West German state, by contrast, has been and continues to be a *Rechtsstaat*—that is, both just and constitutional. Within the rhetoric of this right-wrong dichotomy, certain East German individuals were discredited for not having left the GDR. Because of this failure, they were accused of voluntary alliance with an oppressive and intolerant regime (ibid.). The desired effect, one might speculate, was to marginalize and demean the voices of some East German intellectuals. Given her extraordinary reputation, the most prominent target was possibly Christa Wolf. Most of the attacks against her were voiced and published within the context of the *Literaturstreit*, the literature battle, which, in itself, can be seen as another example of West Germans' desire to establish some form of cultural and/or intellectual hegemony over East Germans.[6]

The *Literaturstreit* roughly coincides with Wolf's publication of *Was bleibt?* (What Remains?) in 1990 and unfolded very publicly in a number of Germany's newspapers and journals. From the beginning, the *Literaturstreit* was not so much about questions of aesthetics, but was a *Kulturgrundsatzdebatte*, a battle about cultural principles (Wittek 11). Instead of creating bridges between East and West, the *Literaturstreit* enlarged the rift between the two groups. Journalists and critics who meant to degrade East German literature and its writers argued that East German literature was created within a coercive system, was subservient to that system, and that, therefore, East German literature does not have any literary value or artistic merit. In "Finding a Place for Christa Wolf," Marjanne Goozé acknowledges the sincerity of the desire to dismiss East German literature when she states that "[a] renewed examination of [Wolf's] literary works . . . serves to counteract the attempted expulsion of GDR writers from the body of German and world literature" (44).

Beyond fame and reputation, there are three other reasons for Christa Wolf's central place in the *Literaturstreit*. First, the publication of *Was bleibt?* (1990) evoked much commentary. Wolf had written the text in 1979, ten years before the collapse of the GDR. The text features a female protagonist who, like many of Wolf's literary characters, is semiautobiographical, and who is coping with an intrusive state surveillance system.[7] Given the date of the work's creation, as well as its content, the critics' response in 1990 was to expose Wolf as an opportunist who casts herself as a victim, or else as a coward who chose to remain silent and not publish her work when it still could have mattered. In Weedon's words, the press accused "Wolf of trying to present herself as both victim and resistance figure, while having failed to contest the regime and fight on behalf of persecuted writers" (224).[8] Second, Wolf's critics found new grounds for accusation when the author's involvement with the *Stasi* (the GDR's state security apparatus) was made public. With this information available, *Was bleibt?* was not only attacked but also ridiculed, and the worthiness of Wolf's work was called into question.[9] Third, Christa Wolf was an ideal target because of her political beliefs. While critical of the GDR, in 1989, she was resistant to "any selling out of the . . . values of the GDR" (Kaufmann, "Developments 212).[10] Along with other East German intellectuals, she had hoped that the collapse of the old regime would be an opportunity to build a new and better socialist state. Within the mainstream discourse of postunification (West) Germany, Wolf's particular beliefs were prone to be marginalized and made Wolf an outsider.

In the early 1990s, Christa Wolf personifies the "exile" in Nico Israel's definition of the term. She is a "coherent subject" not only as a (former) East German citizen but also by virtue of her political convictions. Wolf's new "place" and "home," postunification Germany, appears to have little sympathy and even less use for such East

German attitudes.[11] While exile, or displacement, "wounds people," as Israel writes, "it need not be perceived as a condition of terminal loss" (17). Indeed, as exile denotes pain and loss, it can also mark a departure. Israel explains that "appropriately for a word that . . . derives from the Latin *ex salire*, it [exile] also expresses a sense of 'leaping out' toward something or somewhere, implying a matter of will" (1). Wolf's voluntary and temporary "second exile," to California, appears to lead toward this more positive and constructive sense, for it is in the United States that her next prose work, *Medea*, takes shape. This important text evokes many resonances with the history of the two Germany's and with the author's personal situation. Importantly, *Medea* also offers some thoughts that may influence the Germans' continuing unification and identification within the European community.

Several of Christa Wolf's letters and diary entries during her 1992–93 visit in California express the author's sense of exile and pain (see Hochgeschurz). In a letter from October 1992, for instance, Wolf writes, "[T]he reasons which lead groups of people to depreciate and demonize other people are always the same: ignorance, fear, resistance, a guilty conscience, the need to be exonerated. And this resembles our most recent experiences." It is difficult not to draw a parallel between Wolf's remark about "our most recent experiences" and the implication that it is the East Germans who are members of the "depreciated and demonized" group (presumably by West Germans). The same sources also give indications that the author identifies strongly with certain aspects of Medea's predicament. Witness, for example, Wolf's thoughts about Medea as scapegoat and the way in which she relates Medea to postunification Germany, as well as to her own situation:

> Why do we need sacrifice? Why do we continue to insist on scapegoats. During recent years, after the so-called *Wende* (turning-point) in Germany, which led to the GDR's disappearance from the stage of German history, I saw reason to ponder these questions. Since June 1991, I find in my papers notes about the figure of Medea, who emerged from a context which, for me, was immediate, tumultuous, and dominated by contradictory thoughts and emotions. (Hochgeschurz 21–22)[12]

In another example, Wolf leaves little doubt that she identifies with Medea and writes, "I have been able to empathize with how one must feel when one is rootless" (Hochgeschurz 85).[13] Moreover, one needs to take note that Wolf's interest in the ancient figure is motivated by contemporary problems: "Sometimes, one can clarify contemporary problems by passing them through such seemingly remote figures" (75).[14] Wolf's revelations not only suggest the intellectual and emotional links that exist between the author and her protagonist; they also make *Medea* a relevant commentary on the postunification situation in Germany. In other words, the reader is invited to read *Medea* both as a retelling of a myth and as an allegory of the dramatic changes of the 1990s, because, as Hochgeschurz describes it, "[i]n Christa Wolf's 'different Medea' history and future meet" (7).[15]

One of Wolf's motivations to work with ancient Greek material, especially Euripides's *Medea*, is her interest in how identities and communities are established, how states and civilizations are built, and how the legacy of these processes is passed from one generation to the next.[16] Sometimes, dramatic and sudden changes take place (like the unification of the two German states, for example) that can threaten a community.[17] Such moments are of interest to Wolf because a community (or state) needs to undergo a process of revaluation in order to continue as a continuous community. According to Wolf, the dramatic change that underlies Euripides's work is the shift from a matriarchal to a patriarchal society. In Euripides's drama, the community deals successfully with this change. Yet it does so, in Wolf's view, at great cost, for it requires the complete demonization of Medea, a process during which she becomes the murderess of her own sons and the archetype of the monstrous mother.

Wolf's interest in Medea is to restore some of her humanity.[18] For this reason, it is not surprising that Wolf's Medea murders neither Apsyrtus, her brother, nor Meidos and Pheres, her sons, nor even Glauce, Jason's Corinthian bride. This Medea is a victim of corrupt powers and of individuals who try to protect their own interests. While this is certainly a significant aspect of the text, Wolf's Medea is also, and importantly, an exile. Her situation as exile makes her a unique figure in the text's cast of characters. Her condition as exile allows her to see the vulnerability and arbitrariness of societies and the values with which they identify.

Medea's exile begins with a traumatic experience at Colchis, her homeland: the murder of her brother by a "fanatical band of cronies," who finds Apsyrtos in his bath and kills him while chanting "bloodcurdling songs." Medea explains, "Such was the custom in the olden days, to which, we, too, had appealed because we thought they promised us an advantage. And ever since I shudder at the thought of those old days and the forces they released in us, forces we could no longer control" (Wolf, *Medea* 75).[19] This event makes Medea an exile in that in creates an irreversible break between the subject, Medea, and her context. The paradigm of her native country and its custom of sacrifice does not provide meaning any longer. The loss of meaning is significant for Medea because, as she wonders elsewhere, "[a]nd doesn't everything depend . . . on the significance one gives to an action?" (45).[20] The loss of meaning also prompts Medea to leave Colchis for Corinth.

Initially, Medea believes that Colchis is the "one place in the world where a person can be happy" (Wolf, *Medea* 7).[21] Very quickly, Medea realizes that her first impression was based on ignorance and she comes to realize that Colchis, too, is based on arbitrary values. The worth of a Corinthian citizen, for example, is measured not by his or her character or contribution to society, but by the amount of gold owned (24, 25). More ominously, Corinth is also based on violence and deceit. Akamas, King Creon's first astronomer, explains that Corinth had to change from a matriarchy to a patriarchy in order to remain competitive at a time when more and more patriarchies were being formed around it (95, 116). Akamas thus has no problem rationalizing either the murder of the heir to power, King Creon's daughter Iphinoe, or the subsequent deception of the populace, who are told that Iphinoe had eloped, as unfortunate, but necessary (95, 116).

Because of her singular position as exile and outsider, Medea can perceive the cost at which Corinth (but also Colchis) acquires identity and stability and how the constituent members of the societies are, or choose to be, blind to this cost. Furthermore, Medea realizes that such societies are vulnerable because of an inherent incomprehension of the very possibility of vulnerability. Specifically, the prevalent attitude is that of arrogance, which in turn is based on the (Corinthian) status quo as measure of all things. This is why Medea has a ready answer for Leucon, Creon's second astronomer, when he asks her why Medea sees Corinth on a path toward wreckage: "Your sense of your own superiority, she said. You consider yourselves superior to everyone and everything, and that distorts your vision; you don't see what really is, nor do you see yourselves as you really are" (Wolf, *Medea* 138).[22] To explain any failure, the Corinthians need scapegoats. The Corinthians' sense of superiority leads them to conspire against Medea, and the protagonist, exile and outsider, is driven from the city in the end.

Some critics suggest that Wolf's Medea is capable of her insights because the author "disregards the paradigms of the Colchian and Corinthian cultures" and endows Medea with a "modern psychology" (Wilke 20).[23] Such judgment is significant, for it stresses that Wolf's text is a retelling of the Medea material as well as commentary on contemporary issues. Structurally, therefore, Wolf's *Medea* invites the reader to two different domains. The first is the historical realm (of both ancient Greece and the literary tradition that has contributed to the creation of the Medea myth), while the second is that of modern psychology, feminism, and recent history. It is the second domain, of course, that may reveal some specific connection of Wolf's text to postunification Germany. Indeed, one of the ironies of Christa Wolf's career, as Resch writes, "may well be that her writing will significantly assist the process of a unification she passionately opposed" (171). The concluding section suggests two ways in which Wolf's *Medea* can be read in relation to the unification process. If one agrees that *Medea* comes out of the author's experience of intellectual and artistic exile, one can see how the novel's contributions mark Wolf's departure, her attempt to "leap out" into the future of unifying Germany.

The first of two connections to contemporary issues can be seen in the structure of Wolf's *Medea*, while the second is linked to the author's choice of material for her fiction. Wolf's text falls into 11 sections, each of which represents the monologue of a single voice.[24] While Medea's voice is represented four separate times, more than any other character's voice, it is clear that each of the voices represents a distinct and idiosyncratic *Wahrnehmungshorizont* (horizon of perception). Each voice carries authority on the basis of its existence. If and when such authority is undermined or questioned, it happens through the judgment of another voice. Through the arrangement of voices, Wolf creates a scenario in which individuals are constituent of the community in which they exist and actively contribute to its construction through their utterances. Significantly, the voices in *Medea* are never in dialogue with each other; they either reveal their own thoughts or reproduce another's thoughts in indirect discourse.[25] Here, the implication for a postunification reader is that communities can be built and need not head toward ruin (like Wolf's Colchis and Corinth) if individuals understand that they have a voice (and use it), if the worth of an individual is measured by his or her existence, and if, most importantly, the voices are in dialogue with each other.[26]

The second, indirect implication of Wolf's *Medea* for its postunification audience involves the author's decision to work with ancient Greek material. For Wolf, classical antiquity represents the point of reference for the entire *Abendland* (occident), which has "fed itself" and continues to define its understanding of itself on the basis of classical "ideas, principles of art, political theories, philosophy, and democracy, the great Utopia" (Hochgeschurz 18).[27] Thus the classical culture has been (and is) a productive source for the West's understanding of itself. Read through Wolf's *Medea*, the classical culture, in providing so much, has also obscured its limitations for the West today. Put differently, Wolf's *Medea* is a condemnation of Western culture, which, as Rita Calabrese writes, "has begun in Greece and has taken itself for the absolute measure of humankind" (130).[28] As postunification Germany, in its quest to unify and to create an identity, is paying much attention to the European community, Greek antiquity, the Western heritage, is an important cultural anchor (not only for Germans but for many European peoples). However, Wolf's *Medea* offers an important reminder that no system of values is without weaknesses and that any system of values always comes at a cost, which, if one chooses to ignore it, will bear ruinous consequences.

Notes

1. A sense of displacement is expressed when Wolf, in *Auf dem Weg nach Tabou*, cites a public opinion poll of November 1993, according to which 70 percent of East Germans responded that that which divides Germans outweighs that which unites them (315). In the same work, Wolf talks about a colonization of the East by the West (335). Another term used to describe unification is *annexation* (Resch 161; Kaufmann,

"Developments" 211). Assessing the situation in 1996, Monica Krol qualifies the unification as a "failure" and a "new kind of segregation between East and West" (181). See also Laura Sager's article in which she compares East and West German poetry and shows how the same context (postunification Germany) is expressed very differently by the respective poems—especially with regard to the concepts of identity and community.

2. The experience of loss and alienation on the part of East Germans is generated by the disappearance of the GDR. It is also enhanced by the post-1990 German mainstream discourse. An example is any attempt "to obliterate anything that might have been good about the GDR from public consciousness" (Weedon 224). Alienation of East Germans also occurs in "intercultural" linguistic encounters, in which West Germans are "experts" (and thus in a position of authority and dominance), while East Germans are "novices" (Stevenson 233).

3. With regard to the absence of a single common religion, the two domi-nant religions in Germany were/are Catholicism and Protestantism. For the language issue, see Barbour and his discussion of the fact that not all speakers of German are German citizens; the Austrians and Swiss, for example, speak German as well ("Germany" 159). See Carol Schmid for an interesting investigation of language and identity in Switzerland (123–43). Also, it must be noted that the speakers of German do not all speak the same kind of German, but speak in a number of dialects that vary from country to country and, significantly, within countries.

4. The number of texts dealing with the history of the German states is too vast to consider within the scope of this chapter. I am merely attempting to sketch a general and broad account. Here, I am specifi-cally referring to Barbour ("Germany" 159) and Ruppenthal (15).

5. See Barbour ("Germany" 165), Ruppenthal (15), and Sager (278). With regard to the Germans' interest in the international, especially European, community, after unification as well as before, it is interest-ing to note that in the current *Grundgesetz*, a new article 23 specifies the ways in which the Federal Republic cooperates in the construction of the European Union (22–23).

6. For two different, yet interesting and comprehensive accounts of the *Literaturstreit*, see Thomas Anz's 1995 publication and Bernd Wittek's *Der Literaturstreit*.

7. Many agree that there is a strong and recognizable autobiographical component to Wolf's works in general. Resch describes Wolf as "con-temporary Germany's most autobiographical writer" (170), while Krol qualifies Wolf's writings as "confessional" (119). See also Kaufmann ("Women Writers" 198) and Goozé (45).

8. See also Resch (163, 164).
9. See Wittek. While there seems to be little doubt that Wolf was, at some point, an informer, one needs to keep in mind that the *Stasi* had files on six million people and that, therefore, a significant portion of the population may have been informers and, perhaps even simultaneously, were being informed on.
10. See Christa Wolf's *Reden im Herbst* and *Auf dem Weg nach Tabou*.
11. Regarding reactions to Christa Wolf and those who shared her political outlook, Kaufmann notes that "the various media condemned those writer . . . who had argued against the incorporation of the GDR into the Federal Republic calling them dangerous utopian dreamers, alienated from the ordinary people, intellectuals whose words should be disregarded" (212).
12. "Warum brauchen wir Menschenopfer. Warum brauchen wir immer noch und immer wieder Sündenböcke. In den letzten Jahren, nach der sogenannten 'Wende' in Deutschland, die dazu führte, daß die DDR von der Bühne verschwand, sah ich Grund, über diese Frage nachzudenken. Seit dem Juni 1991 finde ich bei mir Notizen über die Figur der Medea, eine Gestalt, die aus dem aktuellen, für mich sehr aufwühlenden, von widerstreitenden, entgegengesetzten Gefühlen und Überlegungen besetzten Zusammenhang wie von selbst hervortrat."
13. "Ich habe nachempfinden können, wie man sich fühlen muß, wenn man wurzellos ist."
14. "Manchmal kann man an solchen scheinbar weit zurückliegenden Figuren die zeitgenössischen Probleme besonders deutlich herausfiltern." The first time Wolf works with ancient material is in *Kassandra* (1983). In the case of this earlier work, too, there are clear indications that the choice of the author's material is guided by Wolf's concern with modern issues (here: the potentially catastrophic destructive power of nuclear weapons). "Located in the ancient world," Weedon states, "*Kassandra* uses a past setting to raise profound questions about the nature of our present" (236).
15. "[I]n Christa Wolf's 'anderer Medea' begegnen sich Geschichte und Zukunft." In addition to her own reading of *Medea* as postcolonial text, Sabine Wilke gives a good summary of the contexts that have guided interpretations of *Medea*—feminist interests, work on myth, and connection of the novel to contemporary history. Regarding the latter, there is some controversy, and Wilke, among others, dismisses allegorical readings of *Medea*. I agree that many such readings reduce the text to a simple correspondence (in which Colchis stands for the GDR and Corinth for the FRG) and see the text as a mournful

expression of loss. In my opinion, the opposite is the case; that is, while I read *Medea* in connection to contemporary history, I hope to show that the work is very much constructive in that it is forward looking, interested more in the future than in the past.

16. See, for example, Thébaud (591) and Resch (129).

17. See Wolf's letters and diary entries published in Hochgeschurz (esp. 96).

18. This is, of course, the context in which many critics see an identification of Christa Wolf with Medea in which the author portrays herself as unjustly and maliciously demeaned. Some commentators are sympathetic, while others are not. In either case, a reading of Wolf's *Medea* that stops here quite possibly misses the text's more far-reaching contributions.

19. "[S]o ist es Brauch gewesen in den alten Zeiten, auf die auch wir uns ja berufen hatten, weil wir uns einen Vorteil davon versprachen. Und seitdem ist mir ein Schauer geblieben vor diesen alten Zeiten und vor den Kräften, die sie in uns freisetzen und derer wir dann nicht mehr Herr werden können."

20. "[u]nd [kommt] es nicht darauf an, welchen Sinn man einer Handlung [gibt]?"

21. "Ort auf der Welt, da kann der Mensch glücklich sein."

22. "[i]n eurer Selbstüberhebung, sagte sie. Ihr erhebt euch über alles und alle, das verstellt euch den Blick für das, was wirklich ist, auch dafür, wie ihr wirklich seid."

23. See also Ehrhardt (33) and Resch, who describes "the psychological reality behind the tale" to be Wolf's "projection of a contemporary ideal" (120). Although Resch's specific comments apply to Wolf's *Kassandra*, they capture well the dynamics of *Medea*.

24. For a detailed analysis of the voices in Wolf's *Medea*, see Ehrhardt.

25. The prevalence of indirect speech (which reveals as much about the interests of the one reproducing it as it does about the one who is being quoted) is particularly noticeable in the German original, because German verbs take special forms in indirect discourse.

26. See also Wolf's *Hierzulande, Andernorts*.

27. "Ideen, Kunstmaximen, Staatstheorien, Philosophie und [die] große Utopie von Demokratie."

28. "in Griechenland ihren Anfang genommen und sich für das absolute Maß der Menschheit gehalten hat."

Works Cited

Anderson, Benedict. *Imagined Communities*. London: Verso, 1991. Print.

Anz, Thomas, ed. *Es geht nicht um Christa Wolf. Der Literaturstreit im vereinten Deutschland*. Frankfurt am Main: Fischer, 1995. Print.

Barbour, Stephen. "Germany, Austria, Switzerland, Luxembourg: The Total Coincidence of Nations and Speech Communities?" *Language and Nationalism in Europe*. Ed. Stephen Barbour and Cathie Carmichael. Oxford: Oxford UP, 2000. 151–67. Print.

———. "Nationalism, Language, Europe." *Language and Nationalism in Europe*. Ed. Stephen Barbour and Cathie Carmichael. Oxford: Oxford UP, 2000. 1–17. Print.

Calabrese, Rita. "Von der Stimmlosigkeit zum Wort. Medeas lange Reise aus der Antike in die deutsche Kultur." *Christa Wolfs Medea. Voraussetzungen zu einem Text*. Ed. Marianne Hochgeschurz. München: Deutscher Taschenbuch, 2000. 115–47. Print.

Ehrhardt, Marie-Luise. *Christa Wolfs Medea. Eine Gestalt auf der Zeitgrenze*. Würzburg: Königshausen and Neumann, 2000. Print.

Goozé, Marjanne E. "Finding a Place for Christa Wolf: Gendered Identity in *No Place on Earth*." *International Women's Writing, New Landscapes of Identity*. Ed. Anne E. Brown and Marjanne E. Goozé. Westport: Greenwood P, 1995. 44–59. Print.

Grundgesetz für die Bundesrepublik Deutschland. Bonn: Bundeszentrale für politische Bildung, 1990. Print.

Hochgeschurz, Marianne, ed. *Christa Wolfs Medea. Voraussetzungen zu einem Text*. München: Deutscher Taschenbuch, 2000. Print.

———. "Erwünschte Begegnung. Vorwort." *Christa Wolfs Medea. Voraussetzungen zu einem Text*. Ed. Marianne Hochgeschurz. München: Deutscher Taschenbuch, 2000. 7–12. Print.

Israel, Nico. *Outlandish. Writing Between Exile and Diaspora*. Stanford: Stanford UP, 2000. Print.

Kaufmann, Eva. "Women Writers in the GDR, 1945–1989." *Postwar Women's Writing in German*. Ed. Chris Weedon. Providence: Berghahn, 1997. 169–209. Print.

———. "Developments in East German Women's Writing Since Autumn 1989." *Postwar Women's Writing in German*. Ed. Chris Weedon. Providence: Berghahn, 1997. 211–22. Print.

Krol, Monika. "Women Writers and Social Change in the Former GDR after the Wende: Gabriele Stötzer, Christa Wolf and Sarah Kirsch." Diss. U of California P, 1996. Print.

Resch, Margit. *Understanding Christa Wolf. Returning Home to a Foreign Land.* Columbia: U of South Carolina P, 1997. Print.

Ruppenthal, Katrin. *"Zwischen Trauerarbeit und Utopie. Die Auseinandersetzung mit der deutschen Geschichte in der Literatur der DDR."* MA Thesis U of New Mexico, 1999. Print.

Sager, Laura M. "German Reunification: Concepts of Identity in Poetry from the East and West." *The German Quarterly* 76.3 (2003): 273–88. Print.

Schmid, Carol L. *The Politics of Language. Conflict, Identity, and Cultural Pluralism in Comparative Perspective.* Oxford: Oxford UP, 2001. Print.

Stevenson, Patrick. *Language and German Disunity. A Sociolinguistic History of East and West in Germany, 1945–2000.* Oxford: Oxford UP, 2002. Print.

Thébaud, Françoise. "Christa Wolf. The Final Solution." *A History of Women in the West.* Vol. 5. Ed. Georges Duby and Michelle Perrot. Cambridge: Belknap P of Harvard UP, 1994. 591–94. Print.

Weedon, Chris. "Reading Christa Wolf." *Postwar Women's Writing in German.* Ed. Chris Weedon. Providence: Berghahn, 1997. 223–42. Print.

Wilke, Sabine. "Die Konstruktion der wilden Frau. Christa Wolfs Medea Stimmen als postkolonialer Text." *The German Quarterly* 76.1 (2003): 11–24. Print.

Wittek, Bernd. *Der Literaturstreit im sich vereinigenden Deutschland. Eine Analyse des Streits um Christa Wolf und die deutsch-deutsche Gegenwartsliteratur in Zeitungen und Zeitschriften.* Marburg: Tectum, 1997. Print.

Wolf, Christa. *Auf dem Weg nach Tabou. Texte, 1990–1994.* Köln: Kiepenheuer and Witsch, 1994. Print.

———. *Hierzulande, Andernorts. Erzählungen und andere Texte 1994–1998.* München: Deutscher Taschenbuch, 2001. Print.

———. *Kassandra. Vier Vorlesungen. Eine Erzählung.* Berlin: Aufbau, 1983. Print.

———. *Medea. A Modern Retelling.* Trans. John Cullen. New York: Doubleday, 1998. Print.

———. *Medea. Stimmen.* München: Deutscher Taschenbuch, 1996. Print.

———. *Reden im Herbst.* Berlin: Aufbau, 1990. Print.

———. *Was bleibt. Erzählung.* Frankfurt au Main: Luchterhand, 1990. Print.

5

Liberating Mythography

The Intertextual Discourse between Mythological Banishment and Domestic Violence as Exile in *Take My Eyes* (*Te doy mis ojos*)

Maureen Tobin Stanley

Overview

*T*obin Stanley argues that through the intertextual dialogue between the cinematic central plot and mythological stories, which are artistically presented by the masters of Spain's Golden Age, Icíar Bollaín's plot in her film Te doy mis ojos *(Take My Eyes)*[1] becomes one of liberation. Tobin Stanley analyzes a victim's experience of domestic violence as a type of exile. She shows that the Golden Age artworks incorporated by Bollaín invite the viewer to draw parallels between the female lead and the artistic texts. The juxtaposition between the ecclesiastical art and its secular counterparts reflects the tension between, on the one hand, the rigid, hierarchical patriarchal structure of the Roman Catholic Church that prescribes gender norms and, on the other, the sensuality and Kristevian *jouissance depicted in Titian's* Danae recibiendo la lluvia de oro *and Rubens's* Las tres gracias *as well as his* Orfeo y Eurídice. *Baroque art thus becomes a window into two irreconcilable symbolic orders, one of which is the source of the protagonist Pilar's "domestic exile." Through the mythological subjects like exiled Eurydice, Pilar learns that home is found through joy, support, and, most importantly, within herself.*

In *Jung and Feminism—Liberating Archetypes*, Demaris Wehr proposes that feminist appropriation and rewriting of stagnant patriarchal archetypes can lead to a liberating, feminist symbolic order. The film *Take My Eyes/Te doy mis ojos* (winner of seven Goyas),[2] directed by the Spanish actress-turned-filmmaker Icíar Bollaín, explores the intricacies of domestic violence through liberating mythography. By presenting an intertextual dialogue between the cinematic central plot and the mythological stories, artistically presented by the masters of Spain's Golden Age, Bollaín's plot becomes one of liberation. In this study I analyze a victim's experience of domestic violence as a type of exile. The explicit key to exile inherent in the abusive relationship between Antonio and Pilar (respectively played by Luis Tosar and Laia Marull) is Peter Paul Rubens's artistic rendering of Orpheus and Eurydice, a work the protagonist Pilar studies and with which she shares striking similarities. The schizophrenic existence[3] of bliss and pain, "home" and banishment, belonging and marginalization, comfort and fear is evident not only in Eurydice's exile to the underworld but also in Pilar's fractured life. Titian's Danae is also significantly revealing of the inner workings of both Pilar's relationship with Antonio and her own learned identity. Hence the Golden Age artworks incorporated by Bollaín, as objective correlatives, invite the viewer to draw parallels between the female lead and the artistic texts she learns to read.

The juxtaposition between ecclesiastical art and its secular counterparts reflects the tension between, on the one hand, the rigid, hierarchical patriarchal structure of the Roman Catholic Church that prescribes gender norms and, on the other hand, the sensuality, freedom, and Kristevian *jouissance* depicted in Titian's *Danae* and Rubens' *Eurydice* as well as his *Three Graces*. This latter painting, as evident later in this chapter, reflects a model of women's collectivity and friendship that truly makes possible Pilar's liberation from the cycle of abuse. Consequently, the secular and religious artworks contained within *Take My Eyes/Te doy mis ojos* are at odds, just as the female lead's search for self is in conflict with her subordination to her abusive husband.

Violence

Domestic violence is an actuality in Spain. As Bollaín has indicated, cinema "should be a witness to its time and environment . . . [and should also] interpret the emotions of most mortals"[4] (qtd. in Martínez-Carazo 67). *Take My Eyes/Te doy mis ojos* has certainly raised consciousness regarding violence against women. When *Take My Eyes/Te doy mis ojos* was released in 2003, in Spain seventy women were murdered by their partners or ex-partners, fifty thousand domestic abuse charges were filed, and one thousand monthly personal protection orders were granted (Cruz 62). According to Fundación Mujeres's nine-semester study (spanning January 1999 through June 2003), 315 women were murdered by their partners or ex-partners. Each semester, murders increased 9.53 percent, meaning that an average of 2.33 more women are murdered with each subsequent semester. In the first semester of 2003, the number of murdered women (45) is twice the number as those of the first semester studied.[5] In other words, femicide in Spain doubled in a four-and-a-half-year period.

To state the obvious, gender violence is a problem within Spain (not to mention all over the world) that requires complex and creative solutions. Bollaín avers that "el cine es un medio fabuloso . . . si no para denunciar por lo menos para hacer reflexionar" ("cinema is a fabulous means . . . if not to denounce at least to make one reflect") (Camí-Vela 234). Just as the film invites viewers to reflect on gender violence as a grave social issue, so does Golden Age art encourage Pilar to do so within her own life.

Violence as Exile

The condition of exile is that of forced or voluntary removal from one's place or origin. The transitive verb "to exile" is synonymous with "to banish" or "to ostracize." Curiously, the personal noun "exile" connotes an individual who has been banished or ostracized but also a "fugitive" or a "refugee." These flight terms prove most intriguing in that the former entails *fleeing* from the law, whereas the latter entails fleeing from a harmful entity or situation.

The protagonist, Pilar, is an exile for she leaves her marital home. Although she physically leaves of her own accord, it is her husband's vicious abuse that prompts her actions. In this sense, her type of flight makes of her a refugee. Yet within a patriarchal setting, the husband's will is the law of the domestic sphere; hence, Pilar's actions also render her a fugitive.

Bollaín's filmic narrative is as follows. In the dead of night, Pilar and her son have fled their home to seek shelter with Pilar's sister Ana. The following day, when Ana retrieves belongings for Pilar, she comes across accumulated evidence and medical records of sustained and chronic domestic abuse. With Ana's help, Pilar becomes gainfully employed in a museum[6] and, subsequently of her own accord, studies to become an art guide. At work, the protagonist makes many friends who become, along with Ana, a network of support. Pilar's husband, Antonio, begins group sessions for abusive husbands. This prompts Pilar to accept him anew into her life. A romantic courtship ensues, convincing the protagonist to return to the marital home. As Pilar becomes more independent and self-sufficient (both personally and professionally), Antonio increases his verbal, physical, and psychological abuse, which reaches its climax on a day Pilar's professional independence to date also culminated: an interview in Madrid. Following the scene in which Antonio brutally stripped his wife and forced her naked onto the balcony, locking her out of the home, trembling in such fear that she urinated, she attempts to file a police report yet is unable to do so due to lack of contusions. The film concludes with Pilar's brief return to the marital home to retrieve her personal effects, while Antonio, dumbfounded, stares at her as she, with the support of friends, exits his life.

The secular and religious paintings by Golden Age masters (El Greco, Velázquez, Titian, Rubens, Tintoretto, and Ribalta, among others) in Bollaín's film reflect the options available to Pilar, who must choose between, on the one hand, her own needs and developing her talents in order to self-actualize, and, on the other hand, capitulation to her husband's phallocentric desires, thus annihilating her sense of self. Not only is this latter option psychologically and morally crippling, but given the escalating physical abuse, the choice to remain with Antonio would indisputably lead to violence and perhaps death (whether his, hers, or both).

Battered Pilar is not unlike the eighteen million refugees and twenty million displaced peoples (Afkhami, *Women in Exile* vii) who relocate from a caustic place of origin—once called home—to a temporary host environment in hopes of protection and the opportunity to rebuild their lives. Although Pilar is not a displaced geopolitical exile or refugee as are women who cross a national border, she, too, must flee from her home. For Mary Vásquez, "Exile . . . is a specific sort of emigration, and the term does not speak of the other end, the 'entry into' that is immigration. Exile, with its etymological weight of banishment, is a severing, and, even if voluntary, even if sought, carries the connotation of an impetus of some urgency that propels one away, not toward" (14). It is precisely in this sense of banishment, of being propelled away, that we must consider Pilar's exile and that of her mythological counterparts. Through the artworks she studies, because of the mythological subjects like exiled Eurydice, Pilar gleans that to overcome her domestic exile she must find home through joy and support, and, most important, within herself.

Process of Liberation: Recognition, Evolution, and Liberation

As Jacquelin Cruz has succinctly summarized the plot of *Te doy mis ojos*, Pilar "Huye, regresa con su marido y finalmente se libera del todo" (8) ("She flees, returns to her husband and is finally completely liberated"). If domestic abuse can be considered a type of exile, then liberation from the cycle of aggression must be viewed as a quest for and possible attainment of that ineffable psychic notion of being at home, of belonging, and of feeling nurtured. There are seven artworks I have chosen from Bollaín's film: Velázquez's *Cardenal de Borja*, Estévez's *El Cardenal de Borbón*, Titian's *Paulo III*, Luis Morales's *La Dolorosa*, Titian's *Danae recibiendo la lluvia de oro*, and two works by Rubens, *Orfeo y Eurídice* and *Las tres gracias*. Conceptually these works pertain to three categories that reveal a stage in Pilar's process of liberation and subsequent quest for and possible attainment of "home." The works could simply be divided between religious and secular, but upon closer scrutiny, Rubens's *Las tres gracias* stands alone. The three stages in Pilar's psychological itinerary are *Recognition*, *Evolution*, and, finally, *Liberation*. The four ecclesiastical works (three patriarchs and *La Dolorosa*) become a mirror in which Pilar sees herself reflected. With this viewing, she begins to recognize the phallocentric symbolic order that she had internalized and that had been governing her life. The stage I have termed *Evolution* refers to the process of change, self-awareness, and the beginnings of self-definition. It is in Danae and Eurydice that Pilar views beauty and sensuality, traits that the protagonist herself relishes. Yet the pictorial narratives are bittersweet, for joy and passion are intermingled with suffering. The final work, Rubens's *Three Graces*, represents Liberation.

In this film, the viewer's initiation into the world of Golden Age art—a window into two irreconcilable symbolic orders—takes place after the initial film sequence in which Pilar has left Antonio and is living with her sister Ana, a restoration artist at the Catedral Primada de Toledo. Pilar tours the cathedral, and views the portraits of Cardinals Borgia and Bourbon and Pope Paul III, and Morales's *La Dolorosa*. This sequence makes manifest that the Catholic Church is explicitly composed of a hierarchy of powerful men who demand obedience. Within patriarchal order, fear is the motivating force that solidifies the violent hierarchy. Phallocentric symbolic order demands obedience based on fear, and the price for disobedience is retribution or punishment. Fear and suffering are integral to such a worldview, to the point that meaning is conferred upon pain, as is evident in the construct of *la Dolorosa* (Our Lady of Sorrows), which proves not only that womanhood is subordinate to patrilineal order but also that harsh suffering leads to female saintliness. Hence *la Dolorosa* should be considered an explicatory myth that validates and encourages female suffering. By contrast, in a feminist environment, in light of Julia Kristeva's theories on prephallic symbiosis and *jouissance*, collectivity (not hierarchy), joy (not fear), interdependence (not imposition of power), and mutual support (not dominance) reign supreme.

Recognition: Ecclesiastical Patriarchy and the Mother

Yet the martyred mother archetype is key to understanding the plot as well as Pilar's psychological stagnation and subsequent development. If the martyred mother archetype is a behavioral model for Pilar, then, one can say that the female protagonist is an ideal woman for she withstood the suffering imposed upon her by a dominating male figure. Not only does Bollaín present two artistic renditions of the Virgin Mary in the film (Morales's *La Dolorosa* and a detail of El Greco's *El entierro del conde de Orgaz/The Burial of the Count of Orgaz*, in which the Virgin is situated at the right hand of Christ and intercedes in the entry of Orgaz's soul into Heaven), but also the director underscores the verisimilar mother (played by Rosa María Sardà). Pilar's and Ana's own mother embodies the two roles evident in the depictions of the Virgin/Blessed Mother. Sardà's character, an unhappy wife who deferred to her overbearing husband, suffered like *la Dolorosa*. But Bollaín's fictional character also intercedes. She is a mediatrix who insidiously influences her daughters to conform to archaic gender norms. According to Julia Kristeva in her 1975 essay "The Maternal Body," "By giving birth, the woman enters into contact with her mother; she becomes, she is her own mother; they are the same continuity differentiating itself" (Kristeva 303). Hence, as maternity underscores female role models, maternal figures are essential. A woman's identity is based in part on her evaluation of her own matrilineage. To face oneself as a woman is to face one's mother. In Bollaín's film, Pilar certainly confronts her own mother, but also the mother figure the fifth-century preacher Proclus names Theotokos (the God-bearer, the mother of God) (Warner 65). In other words, Pilar faces the icon of *la Dolorosa* and all that she represents.

Let us briefly consider Luis Morales "*El divino*," who exclusively painted Christian subjects for a prescriptive purpose, as Antonio Hernández Sonseca indicates, "to foster religious sentiment, private meditation and public prayer (n. pag.)"[7] Hence Morales's saintly depictions boast a didactic-moral objective and encourage emulation. Sonseca describes Morales's *La Dolorosa* as "a living adoration with marked pathos, [that] radiates vivid anguish and delicate suffering in her gaze" (n. pag.).[8] This vivid anguish and delicate suffering are also evident in Pilar throughout the film.

Kristeva claims that Western artistic depictions of the Mother as subject are a delusion (Kristeva 306) and that Christianity's resorption of femininity is merely a masculine fantasy of the Maternal masking primary narcissism (310). In effect, Antonio's relationship to Pilar is narcissistic for he constantly desires to see himself (and his self-worth) reflected in Pilar. Her view of him is a mirror in which he contemplates himself. When he sees the unconditional acceptance of the pain he causes her, he feels comfort. When she nullifies herself for him, he feels solace. Antonio views Pilar as both his savior and temptress. He believes that both his "attainment" of happiness and his condemnation to despair are contingent on his wife. Clearly, for him, she is both Mary and Eve. She is responsible for his salvation or his fall from grace. Upon close scrutiny, raw misogyny is at the root of this displacement of his fears and desires. As he does/can/will not assume responsibility for his own shortcomings and successes, he projects them onto someone who has vowed to accept (or love) him unconditionally, someone who will take whatever he offers "in sickness and in health (be it mental or other), until death do them part."

Pilar is an outsider in her own body, her own psychic space and clearly her own home, for everyone and everything within it revolves around one individual. Nothing is hers—not her thoughts, not her flesh, not her surroundings. Not unlike a native inhabitant of a ravaged, conquered, and colonized territory, she too has been conquered by desires emanating outside of her. Pilar is an exile within her own home and within her own body. If her body is viewed as reflecting patriarchal, paternal law (wielded by Antonio and all that he represents), then she is excluded from it. It is his, as indicated in the scene in which she gives him as a gift various parts of her anatomy and concludes with "Te doy mis ojos" ("I give you my eyes"). Such relinquishing of self, and particularly self-image/self-perception, together with the recovery of autonomy, are the crux of the film.

The nullification of the feminine self dates back more than two millennia, not just to the Christian figure of the Blessed Mother, but also to her Judaic predecessor, Eve. As Marina Warner considers, Mary is the Second Eve. Eve, mother of the human race sinned, was banished and lost paradise for her progeny, while the second Eve, mother of all Christians, regained paradise (salvation) for all the faithful. If Eve and Mary are the antipodes of the pre-Reformation Christian paradigm for women then it is essential to consider Mary as the anti-Eve. Let us turn to the construct of Eve in order to understand her polar opposite Mary. In Genesis, after Adam blames Eve for succumbing to the serpent's temptation, Yahweh punishes all three. According to the Genesis myth, Yahweh pronounces Eve's punishment: "I will greatly multiply thy sorrow and thy conception . . . and thy desire shall be to thy husband, and he shall rule over thee" (Genesis 3:19, 16 qtd. in Warner 52). If all women are considered "daughters of Eve," then they too (1) suffer, (2) experience painful childbirth, (3) sexually desire their husbands, and (4) are subservient to their spouses' will. Of these four elements, Bollaín portrays three of them in Pilar (suffering, sexual desire for the dominant husband, submissiveness).

As the redemptive daughter the Second Eve, the Virgin Mary, although asexual, still suffers and is submissive (perhaps not to her husband but to the will of God the father). If Mary is a role model, her permutation as Our Lady of Sorrows fuses and exponentially magnifies female suffering as willed by God the father. This gendered anguish determines goodness—in women—to be contingent on their perpetual and limitless acceptance of pain.

Eve's suffering constitutes punishment for herself and half the human race; while Mary's, according to the perverted sadistic imposition and masochistic assumption, is redemptive. Regardless, female suffering is prescribed by both models: saintly mother and condemning temptress. In their chapter titled "Eve and Mary" in *Women in the Middle Ages*, Frances and Joseph Gies claim that "clerical misogyny was as old as the Church" (37). Gies and Gies aver that "[a]t two extremes of its rhetorical needs the Church found two perfect symbols: shallow temptress Eve and immaculate Virgin Mary.[9] The perception of women by medieval churchmen differed little from that of laymen: women were properly subject to men because they were physically and morally vulnerable and lacking in judgment" (41).

Antonio's attitude to Pilar is positively as archaic as in the Middle Ages, a period whose worldview dichotomized femaleness: idealizing impossibly perfect figures and repudiating others. According to Gies and Gies,

Despite such pieties as the *Roman de la Rose*'s "Serve and honor all women," wife-beating was common. "A good woman and a bad one equally require the stick!" ran a Florentine saying. The thirteenth century French law code, *Customs of Beauvais*, stated: "In a number of cases men may be excused for the injuries they inflict on their wives, nor should the law intervene. Provided he neither kills nor maims her, it is legal for a man to beat his wife" . . . An English code of the following century permitted a husband "lawful and reasonable correction." (46)

The religious art referenced in this chapter, although produced in the sixteenth and seventeenth centuries, continues to convey, if I may be so bold, a medieval mindset, in spite of the time period in which it was produced.

What is clear is that a medieval European husband had perfect impunity to brutalize his wife. Twenty-first-century Antonio also boasts impunity. This is evident in two scenes. After Pilar fled her home with nothing but her son and the clothes on her back, her sister, Ana, while gathering Pilar's clothing, comes upon a folder of hospital reports that document the injuries that Pilar had sustained over time as a result of Antonio's rage. Yet these emergency medical visits did not lead to charges being pressed, much less intervention by social services or prosecution. The second scene follows the climax of the film. After having been stripped and humiliated by Antonio on the day she was to interview in Madrid (and thus attain a modicum of financial autonomy), Pilar attempts to file a police report but cannot. When the officer inquires after her injuries, she is forced to reveal that she was only hurting inside. In both these scenes, Bollaín underscores the glaring fact that, without repercussions, a victimizer has no reason to desist the abuse. Taken a step further, one might say that impunity is complicit in the cycle of victimization, for it empowers perpetrators to act on their violent impulses. As an abuser, Antonio feels he is within his rights to brutalize his wife. He is not aggressive toward his boss, nor his brother (with whom he has a very conflicted relationship), nor his clients. Instead, he harms only his wife because there is no social or psychological mechanism in place that effectively deters his aggression. In other words, Antonio fully believes that he is entitled to do as he so chooses with his wife's body—be this to cause her harm or to bring her to orgasm.

Warner's view is that "[b]ecause of the curse of Eve in Eden, the idea of woman's subjection was bound up in Christian thought with her role as mother and temptress" (58). Hence woman is not to be trusted, for she is solely responsible for man's shortcomings, false steps, and failures. She is seen merely as a procreative vessel that produces the father's progeny. Clearly, this is in line with Antonio's regard of Pilar. He implicitly mistrusts her. He also views her as the caretaker of their child, whom he sees only as in relation to himself. Antonio's relationship with their son, Juan, is not based on his desire to fulfill Juan's needs, but rather on his belief that Juan should do and act according to Antonio's own needs, for he is the father. Within a patriarchal domestic sphere, all happenings must revolve around the father.

Evolution: Secular Art

After recognizing the oppressive symbolic order represented by the patriarchal construct of *La Dolorosa* (permutation of the Virgin Mary who is the legacy of Eve), Pilar begins to evolve. Art is a space of refuge, an escape from the microcosm of pain and fear. Curiously the art with which Pilar feels "at home" is humanistic, not religious. If the Virgin Mary (product of the twelfth-century Marian cult) is part of a dichotomy (saintly Mary versus despicable Eve), then the mythical figures of the three Graces, Danae, and Eurydice, cannot be viewed as antithetical to Mary. Rather, they are altogether different, and part of a separate paradigm. By opting to identify with the sensuality evident in mythological subjects of humanistic art, Pilar is liberated from the fear, suffering, and control portrayed in religious iconography and portraiture. Therefore, Pilar has not inverted patriarchal dominance: instead she has subverted it.

The mythical figures (as secular) are not portrayed as concupiscent. Church thought/thinking decrees that sexual pleasure (that is not for the purpose of procreation within marriage) is sinful. According to this line of thinking, sex falls into a binary oppositional paradigm: either sexuality is a means to an end that contributes to the hierarchical power structure, or it is deemed to be evil, a sin, a transgression against an omnipotent patriarchal deity and all his representatives.

Titian's and Rubens's representations of corporality fall outside of the ecclesiastical sexual paradigm, and reveal a new approach to the human form. The voluptuousness, indulgence, and sensuousness speak to a jubilation and celebration of the senses. Aroused Danae, enamored Eurydice, and the dancing Graces—all at home in their nudity—are a far cry from the dark, pain-stricken, fastidiously clothed *Dolorosa*.[10] Pilar comes into contact with the arts and these particular works when she enters the workforce and studies to become a docent. Curiously, just as she analyzes and explicates the humanistic paintings to a class of students, she also teaches us— the viewers and voyeurs of her eye-opening experience—about self-awareness that leads to self-definition. Let us now turn to the myths of Eurydice and Danae whose pictorial forms are vehicles in Pilar's evolution. The nymph Eurydice was married to Orpheus, who upon her death resolved to reclaim her by descending to the underworld, which Hades and Persephone permitted as long as Orpheus did not turn to look at her. When he did, Eurydice vanished (was banished) forever (Graves 198). The parallels between the mythical figures and Bollaín's are essentially the following: the husband's obsession/passion for the wife, her banishment from their shared life, his relentless determination to reunite with her, and, finally, their definitive estrangement, which is a direct result of his lack of self-control.

The myth of Danae is as follows: Acrisius attempts to thwart the prophecy that the son of his daughter, Danae, would murder him. Although Acrisius locks Danae away in a tower/chamber (Graves 105), Zeus frequently enters it as a golden shower and impregnates her with Perseus, who does, in fact, kill his grandfather (186).[11]

The great similarity between Eurydice's tale and that of Danae is that both are banished from a previous original space—home—to another locus not of their choosing by a seemingly all-powerful hegemonic force. Hence both mythological personages experience exile, just as Pilar does when she is ousted from her domestic sphere as a result of Antonio's controlling violence.

While the protagonist explicates Danae's tale at the front of her class, the slide image of Danae is superimposed onto her. As Titian's and Bollaín's subjects overlap and blissfully lift their gazes, while Pilar breathlessly enunciates "Se entrega en cuerpo y en alma" (She gives herself in body and soul), the viewer draws the explicit parallel between the contemporary battered wife and Jupiter's sexual plaything.

Pilar also expounds upon the circumstances surrounding the artwork that Phillip II commissioned from Titian. The painter's 1553 letter to the monarch indicates his intention that the painting "resulte en la habitación donde ha de estar más graciosa a la vista" (should be placed in the [bed]room where it might be most pleasing to the eye).[12] In other words, the painting was for private viewing. At this point Pilar is not only like Danae, whose submission and powerlessness to

Jupiter was complete, but also like the art object, an object herself. Just as Phillip II hid the painting, keeping it only for himself and those within his intimate circle, so did Antonio alienate his wife from all social and family contact, to brand her as his, for his personal satisfaction. Upon seeing Danae who delighted in Jupiter's visits during her captivity, and upon learning the history of the painting's seclusion, Pilar was able to come to grips with the jarring fact that, like Danae and Titian's artwork, she too had been alienated by a domineering male figure that feared losing her to another. "She gives herself in body and soul," states Pilar of Danae's surrender. Key to Pilar's elocution is the present tense of the verb. Danae is not her contemporary, but a mythical figure from over two and a half millennia ago, yet the present tense connotes Pilar's own identification with her. Pilar identifies with *Danae* (the painting) for various reasons and at various levels.

Curiously, the golden shower or golden rain of myth also requires analysis. The sun is a masculine archetype, as well as a divine one. Rain, or water, is a feminine archetype. The golden shower thus becomes an androgynous element—melding the masculine and the feminine—in order to infiltrate the closed feminine space. It is of interest to note that Jupiter's golden shower is strikingly similar to semen, for Danae is impregnated with Perseus subsequent to repeated penetration of the golden rain into this jealously guarded female enclave.

The figure of Danae should not be viewed as dissimilar to that of the Virgin Mary, given the immaculate (i.e., noncoital) conception of a patriarchal deity's male heir. Notwithstanding the similarity between Mary and Danae as humanly untouched reproductive vessels, it is their legacies as adopted, adapted, and perpetuated—by counter-Reformation iconographers such as Luis Morales and Golden Age humanistic painters such as Titian and Rubens—that must be under scrutiny.

Liberation: Seeing Oneself

Nearing the conclusion of the film, Pilar reveals to her sister Ana, "Tengo que verme. No sé quién soy. Hace demasiado tiempo que no me veo" (I need to see myself. I don't know who I am. It has been too long since I have seen myself). The paintings encourage Pilar to *see herself,* to rediscover and remember who she is. Baroque painting is a portal into a paradoxical era of greatness and decline, characterized by *desengaño.*[13] As Pilar becomes undeceived, she is wiser, experiences *desamor,*[14] and is no longer emotionally bound to Antonio. She is positively disillusioned. Her breakthrough is the realization that her pleasure with Antonio—interspersed with fear—was never joy.

Given theories of *l'écriture feminine* (based on Julia Kristeva, Luce Irigaray, Hélène Cixous), female/feminine/gendered writing evinces certain traits, among them writing with the body—with the white ink of mother's milk, or the red ink of menstruation—as well as speaking for oneself. The script by Bollaín and Alicia Luna is clearly a written work, and the film incorporates visual and sound elements. That notwithstanding, Bollaín's filmic text boasts gendered traits. Let us underline that the director/screenwriter is a woman. This fact makes manifest that the filmic narrative of intratextual liberation is interwoven with the extratextual reality of Bollaín's agency, who, as a female active subject is not a muse or a manipulated entity on screen, but rather a gendered being who has seized the reins of creative production.

Furthermore, in line with *l'écriture feminine,* the body, the human form, is essential to the film. Both the female and the male forms are displayed as vital. Although nudity and sexuality take over the big screen, there is no objectification; rather the filmmaker's depiction of the nude human form (other than in the climax of the film) becomes a celebration of both the body and sexuality. These various scenes include Pilar and Antonio's lovemaking during what I term their "courtship period" (when she revels in his attempts to win her over). There is also one fully clothed scene in which the viewer gets a glimpse into the couple's intimate sphere. After one of his outbursts, Antonio leaves just as he is on the brink of violence, and then returns with a gift: an art book. Pilar's receptiveness is extended to her husband interpersonally and also sexually. Her glee at his seemingly thoughtful gift becomes an invitation for him to masturbate her—fully clothed—at the dinner table. Her sexual surrender to him coupled with his ability to almost immediately bring her to orgasm is a dynamic that requires attention. Her receptiveness must be viewed as a forfeiture of limits, or boundaries. Her reaction is viewed by Antonio as carte blanche to do as he pleases, for she is his. It is precisely her unconditional acceptance (hence, lack of limits) that makes possible his dominance over her. Yet her demeanor is only one element in the interrelational dynamic. If Antonio were not bent on controlling her, and did not use his knowledge of her fears and desire to his unfair advantage, then the dynamic of dominance and submission would cease to exist. Thus faithfully depicting an abusive relationship, Bollaín is not dealing in blame. That would have placed all the weight of responsibility on one party and acquitted the other. Rather, Bollaín's masterful portrayal has viewers identifying with both halves of the protagonistic dyad, feeling their pain, empathizing with their fears, and sympathetically reveling in their joy. Cruz observes that the film encourages the viewer's empathy toward Antonio and portrays Pilar as partly responsible for the relationship. She is not a defenseless victim.

Icíar Bollaín's film explores the intricacies of domestic violence by presenting two characters that constitute a protagonistic dyad. Each character is a gendered half of the marital couple. Icíar Bollaín and Alicia Luna's script reveals characters with whom viewers identify. In spite of Pilar's learned helplessness, she is not deemed to be weak. Similarly, although Antonio's mental abuse and violence reach exponential levels, he is not demonized. The filmmakers' *grazia*—to employ a term often used for El Greco, whose home of Toledo is the setting for the film—lies in its ability to illustrate the characters and the plot in such a way that the viewer is moved by and identifies with both the victim and the victimizer. This must be viewed as a feminist strategy. It is phallocentrism that imposes hierarchical binary oppositional thought. Bollaín's approach does not make Antonio an object of blame, but rather treats him as a significant factor in the dynamic. By demonizing him (and correspondingly victimizing Pilar), Bollaín would have annulled Pilar's agency. Only by recognizing her role in the relational dynamic can Pilar engage her own agency and change her situation. According to Cruz, Bollaín's treatment of gender violence is gynocentric, focuses on the female gaze, and clearly demonstrates "the cultural and psychological mechanisms that lead women to see themselves trapped in these types of situations, as well as their responsibility in overcoming them" (68).[15] Although gender violence is misogynistic, Bollaín's portrayal of it is gynocentric, perceived in the feminine and posited in relation to the feminine.

Liberation

Although at first blush, as Cruz observes, the mythological stories that Pilar studies in pictorial fashion are stories that "weave the net that continue to trap her in her relationship with Antonio following their courtship" (77),[16] upon close scrutiny it becomes clear that these tales, sensually depicted, are instrumental in Pilar's liberation. She has learned that, although like Danae and Eurydice she depends on and believes she loves the male figure/s responsible for her banishment/cloistering, she is ultimately responsible for her situation. These sensually depicted tales function as objective correlatives that prompt Pilar to reevaluate her life and ultimately opt for the sensuality, freedom, and collectivity evident in Rubens's *Three Graces*. In fact, the final scene (in which Antonio gazes, through the balcony glass door, at Pilar flanked by her two friends) is an overt nod to Rubens. This polyvalent long shot of the three women, turned away from Antonio, communicates that (1) Pilar has relinquished Antonio and their life together, (2) she is moving forward to begin a new life, (3) she is no longer alienated from social bonds, (4) she is interdependently connected with her friends who support her well-being, and (5), most significant, her friends' gender and number (plural) provide an alternative to hierarchical phallocentric structure. Susan Martin-Márquez has observed that Bollaín's female characters "learn to nurture each other" (259) and "offer an intriguing perspective of the future of 'home-making' in Spain" (257). Pilar, prodigy of *La Dolorosa* and an exile in an abusive patriarchal domestic setting, sees herself in Golden Age depictions of classical and Christian myths, is subsequently liberated from the cycle of violence, and, finally, looks toward the future where home resides in the nurturing psychic space of interdependence and friendship.

By leaving the phallocentric, patriarchal domestic sphere and resting in an altogether different symbolic order in which *jouissance* reigns supreme, Pilar has founded the psychic space of home. No longer banished like Eurydice, nor cloistered like Danae, nor living within inner exile in her own domicile, Pilar's sense of belonging resides and is rooted in her own self-definition that resulted from her ability to see herself. Pilar's articulated self-awareness—"I need to see myself. I don't know who I am. It has been too long since I have seen myself"—must be viewed by Bollaín's viewing/voyeuristic public as a manifesto of sorts, a proclamation to emancipate by regarding oneself on one's own terms. In the end, Pilar does see herself, comes to know who she is, and inaugurates an era in which, as a woman, her self-reflexive gaze is decidedly gynocentric.

Notes

1. A note should be made regarding a small discrepancy. The film in English is known as *Take My Eyes*, yet the Spanish title literally translates as "I give you my eyes." The English translation of the title eliminates the agency of the first-person subject, establishes an implicit second-person subject, and changes the mood from the indicative to the imperative.

2. Best picture, best script, best director, best female lead, best female supporting role, best male lead, best sound.

3. Marjorie Agosín has characterized exile: "Perhaps it is a schizophrenic existence" (Agosín 148).

4. "debe ser testigo del su tiempo y su entorno . . . [además de] interpretar los sentimientos del común de los mortales" (quoted in Martínez-Carazo 67, my translation).

5. See Fundación Mujeres (n.pag.).

6. Here, there is a bit of artistic license as it appears that the protagonist will be working at the Catedral Primada, where her sister restores artworks (some of which are necessarily and creatively misrepresented in locations other than their actual locations in order to carry the plot forward) and where many of the artworks depicted are housed. Nonetheless, it also appears that Pilar works in Santo Tomé. Regardless of the creative license taken with actual spaces of religious art, the plot is seamless and stresses the link between Pilar's development and viewing/reading/understanding art.

7. "[P]ara fomentar el sentimiento religioso, la meditación privada y el rezo público" (my translation).

8. "[U]na plegaria viviente con acentuado patetismo, [que] irradia en su mirada una congoja viva y un dolor delicado" (my translation).

9. The Immaculate Conception became dogma in 1854 (Kristeva 315).

10. Fittingly, Our Lady of Sorrows is the mother of the *massa peccati* that constitutes the human race, plagued by and condemned to original sin, a doctrine defined by St. Augustine at the end of the fourth century (Warner 53).

11. "Se representa aquí la fábula mitológica que relata cómo Zeus se transformó en lluvia de oro para seducir a la bella Dánae, a la que su padre tenía encerrada en una cámara herméticamente cerrada, para

guardarla de las acechanzas del dios o de cualquier otro mortal que se le aproximara. En sus aventuras galantes, Zeus se metamorfoseaba para evitar ser reconocido: en águila, en toro, en cisne . . . , o en lluvia de oro, como en este caso. De esta especial relación con Dánae nació Perseo, uno de los héroes más importantes de la mitología clásica" (http://museoprado.mcu.es/cuadro_diciembre_2003.html).

12. http://museoprado.mcu.es/cuadro_diciembre_2003.html.
13. Desengaño cannot be translated but can be described as an "awakening to the nature of reality[,] . . . waking to true awareness . . . [,] to have the scales fall from one's eyes . . . Such a . . . desirable . . . [d]isillusionment comes to be . . . venerated, as a sort of wisdom" (Green 143).
14. There is no perfect translation for the term "desamor." It is the opposite of "amor" (love), yet does not connote hate. It could be described as the process of falling out of love, of becoming disillusioned with the object of one's desire.
15. "[L]os mecanismos culturales y psicológicos que conducen a las mujeres a verse atrapadas en este tipo de situaciones, así como su responsabilidad . . . en la superación de las mismas."
16. "[T]eje[n] la red que la vuelve a atrapar en la relación con Antonio tras su perseverante 'cortejo.'"

Works Cited

Afkhami, Mahnaz, ed. *Women in Exile: Feminist Issues: Practice, Politics, Theory.* Charlottesville: UP of Virginia, 1994. Print.

Agosín, Marjorie. "I Invented a Country." *Women in Exile: Feminist Issues: Practice, Politics, Theory.* Ed. Mahnaz Afkhami. Charlottesville: UP of Virginia. 140–49. Print.

Bollaín, Icíar. *Take My Eyes/Te doy mis ojos.* Alta Producción. 2003.

Camí-Vela, María. "Una entrevista con Icíar Bollaín." *Cine-Lit 2000: Essays on Hispanic Film and Fiction.* Ed. George Cabello-Castellet, Jaume Martí-Olivella, and Guy H. Wood. Corvallis: Oregon State U, 2000. 232–43. Print.

Cruz, Jacqueline. "Amores que matan: Dulce Chacón, Icíar Bollaín y la violencia de género." *Letras Hispanas* 3.1 (Spring 2005): 67–81. Print.

Fundación Mujeres. *Informe sobre violencia contra las mujeres en España Tasas y tendencias de Homicidio/Asesinato 1999/2003.* Web. <http://www.redfeminista.org/nueva/uploads/Informe_Fundacion_Mujeres.pdf>

Gies, Frances, and Joseph Gies. *Women in the Middle Ages.* New York: Harper and Row, 1978. Print.

Graves, Robert. *The Larousse Encyclopedia of Mythology.* New York: Barnes and Noble, 1994. Print.

Green, Otis. *The Literary Mind of Medieval and Renaissance Spain.* Lexington: UP of Kentucky, 1970. Print.

Hernández Sonseca, Antonio. *Pintura en la Catedral de Toledo.* <http://www.architoledo.org/catedral/pintura/default.htm>.

Kristeva, Julia. *The Portable Kristeva.* Ed. Kelly Oliver. New York: Columbia UP, 1997. Print.

Martin-Márquez, Susan. "A World of Difference in Home-making: The Films of Icíar Bollaín." *Women's Narrative and Film in 20th Century Spain.* Ed. Kathleen Glenn and Ofelia Ferrán. New York: Routledge, 2002. 256–72. Print.

Martínez-Carazo, Cristina. "*Flores de otro mundo*: La pluralidad cultural como propuesta." *Letras Peninsulares* 15.2 (Fall 2002): 377–89. Print.

Nair, Parvati. "Transculturality, Deteriorization and the Question of Community in Icíar Bollaín's *Flores de otro mundo.*" *Post Script* 21.2 (Winter–Spring 2002): 38 (13). Print. <http://find.galegroup.com/itx>.

Oliver, Kelly, ed. *The Portable Kristeva.* New York: Columbia UP, 1997. Print.

Vásquez, Mary. "The Grammar of Contested Memory: The Representation of Exile in Selected Female-Authored Texts of Diaspora." *Female Exiles in Twentieth and Twenty-first Century Europe.* Ed. Maureen Tobin Stanley and Gesa Zinn. New York: Palgrave MacMillan, 2007. 13–29. Print.

Warner, Marina. *Alone of all Her Sex.* New York: Knopf, 1976. Print.

Wehr, Demaris. *Jung and Feminism—Liberating Archetypes.* London: Routledge, 1988. Print.

6

Souls in Transit

Exilic Journeys in Fatih Akin's
The Edge of Heaven (2007)

Gesa Zinn

Overview

In Fatih Akin's film The Edge of Heaven,[1] *the main characters engage in various exilic journeys on their way to self-discovery. Departing from death/pain, their travels take them to new places both outwardly and within. Foreigners to others and to themselves, they live in limbo, outside the mythical circle of life, a state viewers of the films are able to experience because of the space and time configurations of Akin's film text, which invokes in them the notion of diaspora (*Zerstreuung*). Through the characters' criss-crossings and other spatial and temporal markers,* The Edge of Heaven *heightens the very space of transit and transition. Typical of many films including the genre of the* road movie, *from which Akin borrows, this film does not emphasize the female traveling experience, but it does underline women's souls transitioning and arriving at a new "home," something denied the male protagonist, Nejat Aksu, who, as the foreigner, never arrives.*

Many exiles are not exiles by choice but refugees who migrate as a result of natural catastrophes or persecution; there are also those who leave their homes voluntarily. They depart to be with loved ones or to leave or return to their past, or they may depart to (re)discover themselves. Whereas there are many motives and explanations as to why people undertake exilic journeys, the outcomes of their travels are often very similar. According to Susan L. Roberson, who has written extensively on the anthropology of travel writing, "[f]or those who travel or do not experience the trauma of being violently uprooted, travel can facilitate more positive self-transformations. Indeed, it is an axiom of travel theory that with journeying one's sense of self changes, transforms as the wayfarer finds inner resources and matures" (Roberson xvii). Traveling, then, frequently leads to character transformations that bring about a more developed "I," and nowhere is that more visible than in *The Edge of Heaven*, one of the latest films by the German-Turkish filmmaker Fatih Akin. In this film, German and Turkish migrants cross the borders that separate Turkey and the Federal Republic of Germany many times.

The results of these criss-crossings are closely examined in this chapter, along with the causes for the inner and outer journeys that impact and inform the characters' personal development. While my main discussion focuses on Nejat Aksu (played by Baki Davrak), the lead role in this film, it is the female characters, and among them especially Susanne Staub (Hanna Schygulla) and Ayten Oztürk, also known as Gül (Nurgül Yesilçay), who change and grow and ultimately become part of their new environment. I argue that their exilic journeys lead them to a new beginning. Unlike Nejat, the endlessly traveling male, they eventually arrive.

The Edge of Heaven: Summary

Fatih Akin's film opens outside a gas station where the main character, Nejat Aksu, pulls up to buy gas, food, and water before heading back onto the road. In the next shot, we find ourselves in the city of Bremen, Germany, in which a protest march is taking place. It is May 1, International Worker's Day. Ali Aksu (Tunkel Kurtiz), Nejat's father, is walking by, smiling. Ultimately he ends up in a red-light district in which he makes first contact with Jessy, alias Yeter (Nursel Köse). Yeter eventually moves in with him, which comes as a surprise to his son, Nejat, an academic and scholar of German literature at the University of Hamburg. During Nejat's first and second visits to his father's apartment, as well as during their visits to Ali in the hospital, Nejat and Yeter get to know and grow fond of each other. Nejat, for example, finds out that she is Turkish and that she sends money home to Turkey for her daughter's university studies. Their bilingualism connects them as well. Both are able to speak either German or Turkish, indicating their familiarity with both languages, which sets them apart from, for example, Ali or the two Turkish-Muslim men who approach Yeter and force her to live a more decent life, "appropriate" for a Turkish woman. Yeter's sudden death, a result of an argument between her and Ali, comes as another big surprise to Nejat and distances father and son even further. Nejat eventually travels to Istanbul in search of Yeter's daughter, Ayten, in order to pay for her university education. Little does he know that she had fled the Turkish police to find asylum in Germany. While in Bremen, Ayten is befriended by a young woman, Charlotte, who invites the rebellious young Turkish woman to stay in her home, an invitation Charlotte's mother, Susanne, does not find particularly pleasing. When Ayten is arrested and her asylum plea is denied, she is deported and imprisoned in Turkey. Charlotte travels to Istanbul in an attempt to have her friend released from prison, but she finds that in this new and foreign environment, with different laws and customs, it is difficult to visit her. Eventually, Charlotte meets her untimely demise in an attempt to retrieve her stolen purse from a gang of teenage street punks. Her purse contains Ayten's gun, which Charlotte promised to hide so that neither the police nor other gang members of Ayten's rebel group could find it. Charlotte is killed at point-blank range by one of the young thugs, who is unwilling to give her back her belongings.

Susanne soon leaves for Istanbul to take care of her daughter's belongings and to be close to her. At approximately the same time, Ali, who has been deported from Germany after having served a jail sentence for killing Yeter, arrives in Istanbul to continue his travels to the Black Sea. In Istanbul, Susanne moves first into a hotel room and then into Charlotte's apartment, which Charlotte had been renting from Nejat, who had previously moved to Istanbul to search for Ayten. Unable to find her, he decided to stay in the city and buy a German bookstore. Nejat, upon meeting Susanne and thinking about his relationship with his father, goes to his father's hometown in hopes of meeting him there. Susanne, in fulfilling her daughter's wishes, is able to have Ayten released from prison. Overcoming their differences in light of Charlotte's death, Susanne and Ayten each start a new life in Istanbul, leaving their pasts behind.

Life and Death as Nodal Points of Exilic Journeys

Homi Bhabha, who has written extensively about exile experiences, characterizes the life of an exile as a never-ending story, one that lacks a beginning and an end:

> The "beyond" is neither a new horizon, nor a leaving behind of the past . . . Beginnings and endings may be the sustaining myths of the middle years; but in the fin de siècle, we find ourselves in the moment of transit where space and time cross to produce complex figures of difference and identity, past and present, inside and outside, inclusion and exclusion. (Bhabha 217)

On the Other Side, which is a direct translation of the film's German title, *Auf der Anderen Seite*, can be read as a reference to the characters' travels from place A to place B, in this case outer journeys from Germany to Turkey or vice versa. It is interesting to note, however, that the characters' travels are not one-way excursions or the usual "return home" as in films that deal with displacement and in which the displaced actually arrive "home" (Naficy 68). *The Edge of Heaven* not only shows film characters traveling back and forth between Bremen and Istanbul; it also makes a special effort to highlight their crossings by showing airports, runways, and passport offices, frequently by setting up parallel structures between arrivals and departures. For example, in just one shot we see Susanne arriving at the airport in Istanbul and Ali returning to his home country after having been deported from Germany. We also see close-ups of a casket (Yeter's) leaving the airport in Germany and arriving in Istanbul. Barbara Mennel discusses these numerous crosscuttings in detail in her article "Criss-Crossing in Global Space and Time." She makes the point that in Akin's film, which deals with a younger generation of Turkish immigrants to Germany than do the films discussed in Hamid Naficy's book about exile and alienation in cinema, repeated displacements take place, underlining Homi Bhabha's point that transit—the crossing of space and time—produces complex characters of difference and identity. These outer journeys, however, have stories—inner journeys—which are unique to every character and aid in their growth as human beings. In traveling across to the other side, for example, the characters get in touch with themselves and discover their inner selves, much like the protagonists of the *Bildungsroman*, a nineteenth-century German novel of all-around self-development that can be read as an "apprenticeship to life" or a "search for meaningful existence within society."² Needless to say, migrating from one place and one time to another influences their life experiences, coloring their self-development as truly exilic. Thus their living begins with their inner journeys, exile experiences in which they confront the "stranger" and "strangeness" within themselves. In the *Bildungsroman* a loss or discontent serves as the catalyst for self-discovery. Similarly, Fatih Akin chooses the experience of death as the root of his characters' stories in *The Edge of Heaven*. As the other side of life, death challenges living for those suddenly touched by the death of a loved one. Paradoxically, it is the exiles' experience of death that catapults them into living—into not only accepting the cards they have been dealt but also finding themselves.

The film introduces death and love/life in the beginning when the main character, Nejat, travels through a small Turkish town. As he stops for fuel and enters the gas station, the song "Ben seni sevdigimi" plays inside the gas station's store. The singer is the famous Kazim Kojuncu, who died early in life, as the gas station attendant informs Nejat, who is unfamiliar with both the love song (translation: "I love you") and the singer. Death and love thus close together foreshadow Nejat's outer and inner journeys, which he has just begun. His traveling story is presented as a narrative that starts where his journey eventually ends, or so it seems, presenting life as an apparent circle.

The Exilic Experience: Souls in Transit

"To be in exile means to be out of place; also, needing to be rather elsewhere; also, not having that 'elsewhere' where one would rather be. Thus, exile is a place of compulsory confinement, but also an unreal place, a place that is itself out of place in the order of things," states Zygmunt Baumann (Baumann 1). To understand this unreal place that is itself out of place in the order of things, it is helpful to look at some characteristics of exile and of the foreigner whom the linguist, psychoanalyst, and critical theorist Julia Kristeva describes in her text *Strangers to Ourselves*. For example, she mentions that not only does exile always involve a shattering of the former body, but it also shatters all sense of belonging (Kristeva 30). Furthermore, the exile, the foreigner, is aloof. She or he does not belong to any place, any time, or any love: "A lost origin, the impossibility to take root, a rummaging memory, the present in abeyance. The space of the foreigner is a moving train, a plane in flight, the very transition that precludes stopping" (Kristeva 7–8). It is thus no surprise that we see the main character of *The Edge of Heaven* traveling in many parts of the film. Indeed, in one of the first sequences depicting him, Nejat, who is rather heavy hearted, travels by train and streetcar between the University of Hamburg and his father's apartment in Bremen. He, being a German with a second-generation Turkish background, has climbed up the social ladder and become integrated into German society, or so it seems: his educational background as an academic at the University of Hamburg sets him apart from his father, a first-generation immigrant, who most likely arrived with the many other guest workers Germany invited in the second half of the 1950s.[3] Needless to say, Nejat has little in common with his father, who frequents the brothels as well as the racetrack where he bets on the horses. Socioeconomically and educationally, father and son, as could be expected, are at odds with each other.

Nejat

In coming to terms with the changes in his short life as a scholar of German literature and culture, changes brought about not only by events triggered by his father's unintentional killing of Yeter but also by a general feeling of discontent, Nejat is what the psychoanalyst Julia Kristeva calls the foreigner per se, the one never at home, the endless searcher and finally traveler who confronts the foreigner inside himself. He comes close to what Edward Said calls a writer-in-exile (an intellectual) in that his estrangement is felt not only at the personal level. Like Said's intellectual exile, he is a person at odds with his society; he has a double perspective in that he does not see things in isolation, and he can never fully arrive. In his essay "Intellectual Exile: Expatriates and Marginals," Said writes that becoming an expatriate, migrant, or immigrant (i.e., an exile) is based on different relations to one's homeland. Nejat's relationship to Germany is, I argue, changing as he is changing, as he contemplates if either evolution or revolution moves humankind forward.

Of all the characters in the films, Nejat is the most developed as an alien, a foreigner. At first sight, as a bilingual and bicultural

German, he may even be the most adapted/integrated foreigner. Yet paradoxically, he barely fits in because no matter how well he adapted to the German language and culture—he is professor of German language and culture after all—his inner journey pulls him away from it, back to Turkey, where his roots are. There is also his desire to come closer to "the other side" (as the original German title indicates), the other half of his soul he left behind. It is this other side that brings him closer to his father, Ali, who returns to his roots after being expelled from and thus estranged by German society. There is the estrangement from his father as well, which we witness a few times during the film. After all, his father has a mistress who is a prostitute; moreover, he asks Nejat some rather crass personal questions (for instance, "Who are you fucking now?") out of the blue, as he drops him off at the train station. And there is Ali's over-all patriarchal behavior, his attempt to control Nejat, and, moreover, Yeter. Nevertheless, Nejat slowly but surely finds his way back to Ali, although he never truly connects with him.

Intertextuality

When Nejat arrives at his father's apartment in the north-German city of Bremen, he hands him a present: a book by Selim Özdo-gan titled *Demicinin Kizi* (in German: *Die Tochter des Schmieds*; in English: *The Blacksmith's Daughter*). Written in 2007, it is the story about Gül, a girl who grows up in Turkey in the 1950s and leaves for Germany as a young woman. Her father's new wife, Arzu, gives birth shortly after Gül's mother dies. It is the first boy in the family. Gül and her sisters are sent to the other room of their summer home while their stepmother is in labor. The three sisters, Gül, Melike, and Sibel, are fighting while Arzu is having her baby. Melike, Sibel, and Timur, their father, cannot believe how badly Gül gets hurt during the fight, and Timur wants to take Gül to the hospital. But his wife prevents him from doing so, saying that everyone will think that it was he who hurt her. In her pain, Gül remembers,

> Her father had slaughtered a lamb. She'd felt sorry for the animal, but she felt neither fear nor revulsion and knew very well that she would eat its meat later on. Timor bled the lamb and chopped it into sections. Part of one leg was in a large basin, and the muscles

started to twitch, tensing and relaxing in quick succession. That was the moment when Gül became frightened because there appeared to be life where none should be. She had stared at the leg, not daring to touch it, although she wanted to do just that. And this pain is exactly the same. It exists independently of Gül, it is bigger than her, encasing her. (Özdogan 6)

For Nejat, the book is a way to tell his father about himself: his feeling neglected, perhaps, while they still lived in Turkey. And the book is also a subtext for Ayten/Gül, as she has the same name as the girl in the book who, moreover, was also left behind by her mother, who also traveled to Germany.[4] The parallels between the two texts are striking, including the emphasis on pain, which both Güls experience.

Ayten (Gül)

As we find out later in the film, pain is as much a catalyst for the journeys of all Akin's characters as it is for Özdogan's Gül who leaves Turkey to travel to Germany. Her namesake in *The Edge of Heaven*, for instance, escapes Istanbul as a terrorist wanted by the authorities in her home country. In search of her mother, who has been living in Bremen for many years but with whom she seems to have little contact, Ayten/Gül, the illegal immigrant, meets Charlotte, a student at the University of Bremen. After spending many happy days together—Charlotte offers Ayten/Gül a place to stay at her mother's house—they fall in love. Yet their time together is short as Ayten/Gül is denied asylum and deported to Turkey, where she is incarcerated in a women's prison with a possible sentence of up to 23 years.

Ayten's/Gül's pain is most visible when she enters the building reserved for asylum seekers in the city of Bremen for the first time. Her room is bare, with just the essentials: a bed, a table, a chair. A visitor is only allowed to spend three nights a month with her. This bleakness, coupled with the possibility of being deported to Turkey where major criminal charges would be brought against her, and the prospect of being separated from Charlotte are too much for her. Ayten/Gül, otherwise tough, daring, and determined, falls apart: she sits on her bed, crying. Reaching out to Charlotte, who gives her her hand and embraces her, Ayten/Gül slowly gains composure, yet acknowledges defeat: she may lose her girlfriend and her "safe h(e)aven."

This is the only time in the film where Ayten/Gül, the idealist fighting against poverty, and for freedom, equality, and education of the masses in the streets of Istanbul, is afraid, truly scared. Her values she can defend in theory only because she does not connect to anyone, such as a relative or friend in poverty or any other human being who is unable to be "free" as a result of his or her class background or lack of education. Armed with a gun as well as her noble values, Ayten/Gül leads the life not only of a revolutionary but of a terrorist as well, hurting others whose pain she can neither feel nor foresee, as these people are abstract, unreal, and have no connection to her. Yet having met Charlotte and having experienced the "human touch," the love of and for a girlfriend, just like Gül in the novel *Die Tochter des Schmieds*, she suddenly discovers that "there was life where none should be": Charlotte. And just as Gül in the novel wants to touch the leg of the lamb, so Ayten/Gül in the film searches for Charlotte's hand, and finds it while sitting on the bed; she is truly a foreigner in the asylum seekers' home in the Federal Republic of Germany, waiting for "judgment day." Pain, her pain, just like little Gül's pain in Özdogan's novel, is the language her body speaks, reacting to trauma.

The linguist, psychoanalyst, and critical theorist Julia Kristeva speaks of a secret wound, often unknown to himself, that drives the foreigner to wandering. "Poorly loved . . . he does not acknowledge it" (Kristeva 5). Nejat, discontented with his life in Germany, is on the move, searching for his "lost father." Like Nejat, Ayten/Gül, left behind by her mother who had immigrated to Germany as a guest worker, seeks shelter and love in an organization of idealistic yet aggressive women who have become hardened as a result of being ostracized by their motherland Turkey. Ayten/Gül, who resembles a threatening alien from another place, comes close to this image: she is armed, on the run, has terrorist leanings, and is from a non-Western (or only half Western) country with a predominantly Muslim population. Yet Akin allows this character much more depth than the above description warrants. He shows her as alienated from her own society, a woman on the fringes who does not support her society's values but in fact chooses violence to battle against them. Living and working at the periphery of Turkish society, she is, in a sense, a foreigner within her own home, Turkey.[5] And it is her journey to Germany that changes her, softens her, while she engages with human beings—foreigners to her—in a more civil even loving way than she does with her own people. Kristeva writes the following about the particular type of foreigner she refers to as *fanaticist*— namely, that the

> hardness which characterizes him or her is in a state of weightlessness as an absolute that does not last, for as soon as [these] foreigners have an action or a passion, they take root. Temporarily, . . . , but intensely . . . The flame that betrays his latent fanaticism shows only when he becomes attached—to a cause, to a job, to a person. What he finds there is more than a country; it is a fusion, in which there are not two beings, there is but a single one who is consumed, complete, annihilated . . . all foreigners who have made a choice add to their passion for indifference a fervent extremism that reveals the origins of their exile. For it is on account of having no one at home against whom to vent their fury, their conflagration of love and hatred, and of finding the strength not to give in to it, that they wander about the world, neutral but solaced for having developed an interior distance from the fire and ice that had seared them in the past. (*Portable Kristeva* 270, 271)

I argue that Ayten/Gül, Yeter's daughter, is the "fanatic foreigner" Kristeva describes, for, over time, and the more she gets to know Charlotte, the university student from Bremen, her standoffish, brusque, and almost cold disposition diminishes and the former revolutionary, the rebel, shows her softer side as she discovers her love for Charlotte. Later on, Ayten/Gül serves time in a women's prison, and from prison she even reaches out to Susanne, Charlotte's mother, with whom she had not been getting along in Germany. In a gesture to heal the wound that opened up after Charlotte's death, she embraces Susanne, who, too, warms up to her daughter's girlfriend. She also leaves her former life as a terrorist behind (much to the dismay of her imprisoned group leader) and begins to embrace humanity. At the end of her journey, as her name indicates, she turns from Ayten into Gül, a rose that blossoms.[6]

Nejat and Ayten/Gül: Two Opposites and Opposing Forces

Like Ayten, changing into Gül as a result of confronting strangers and strangeness in life, Nejat undergoes a transformation as well; his, however, takes place over time and appears to be connected to his estrangement not only from his biological father but also from one of Germany's father figures, the well-known writer Johann Wolfgang von Goethe. Two scenes in the film that stand out in this regard show Nejat lecturing on Goethe's ideas about evolution. In my opinion, Nejat distances himself from Goethe's endorsement of evolution over revolution when, soon after this lecture, he "takes action," initiating changes in his life by physically and mentally crossing borders to become closer to his father and his home. Interestingly, his lecture on Goethe's philosophy about evolution—"Who would want to see a rose bloom in winter?"—is shown twice in the film, and both times Ayten/Gül is present in the lecture hall. In one of the key scenes, the subject matter of Goethe's text, the rose, is, among other references, a reference to Gül, whose name translates into "rose." Moreover, the "lecture shots" are set up to contrast Nejat and Gül cinematographically. Mennel writes, "The first of the two shots begins with the camera focusing on Nejat lecturing [and] then move[s] to Ayten sleeping in a seat in the foreground of the shot while Nejat is positioned out of focus in the background and then moves onto Nejat lecturing. Thus, both scenes temporally overlap but advance in Nejat's lecture: repetition with a difference, or to put it differently: a minor narrative advancement that results from a temporal overlap" (Mennel 16).

In these scenes we have a revolutionary figure—Ayten/Gül, the terrorist/activist—facing Nejat, up until his change as a proponent of evolution, as it appears that he was rather content in teaching Goethe's evolutionary worldview following exact and consistent rules (Martens n.p.). In line with Goethe, Nejat lectures that everything has its orderly place in the world: "Who would want to see a rose bloom in the depth of winter? Everything has to take its time: leaves, buds, blooms . . . Only the fool demands this non-temporal intoxication" (Martens n.p., qtd. in Mennel 15). Helge Martens goes on to explain that Goethe was appalled by a lack of rules: death, the unstructured world of mountains. "The evolutionary creation through water and in phases and rules following consistent laws was his model of growth."[7] Relying on Martens, Mennel elaborates on the two schools of thought that were prevalent during Goethe's time and that, it appears, are represented by Nejat and Ayten/Gül: the Neptunists and the Plutonists. Named after the Roman god of the sea, Neptune, the Neptunists believed that "all geological sedimentation was sedimentation from the ocean." Named after the Roman god of metals and the underworld, Pluto, the Plutonists believed that "geological stratification resulted from sedimentation from different mountain formations." Neptune and water, according to Mennel, stood for evolution, Pluto and volcanoes for revolution (Mennel 16). As Mennel concludes, Nejat, ending at the ocean, embodies evolution, and Ayten endorses revolution (ibid.).

Yet there is a tendency to break up this binary, this set of opposites, in that Ayten's/Gül's aggressiveness diminishes throughout her journey and Nejat's motivation and actions inducing changes increase, even though he stops short of becoming a revolutionary. Yet, like a revolutionary anarchist, he crosses national and cultural borders and hovers at the edge of society/civilization at the film's end. Unlike Ayten's/Gül's, however, his revolution turns inward.

These scenes in the university lecture hall are the highlight and turning points of the film. Not only do they continue the "dialog" about protests and protesting; that is, concerning social change—be it evolution or revolution (introduced early in the opening scene in which Ali walks by a May Day demonstration in Berlin, smiling); they also represent the beginning of personal changes for Ayten/Gül and Nejat. For Ayten/Gül, who was a militant activist in a demonstration in Istanbul prior to coming to Germany, her lying passively across the table during Nejat's lecture shows us the softening of her nature mentioned earlier. She seems subdued. Having found friendship and love, which have been slowly evolving during her spring/summer stay in Germany, her former aggressiveness has given way to humanism; she truly begins to blossom into a rose. This *Frühlingserwachen* (spring awakening), following dreadful months of dreary weather (fall/winter in northern Germany), takes place in Nejat as well, but in the opposite direction. He decides to leave his "passive life" (he earns his livelihood by discussing ideas) behind and become (physically) active in finding himself: (a) on the road, (b) seeing to it that Yeter is buried, (c) attempting to finance her daughter's education, (d) buying a German bookstore in Istanbul (his lifeline: his German baggage/culture in tow), and (e) reaching out to his father after Susanne, Charlotte's mother, points him in the right direction. Between the two, Nejat and Ayten/Gül, a crossing-over, a chiasma, takes place, adding another to the many cinematographic chiasmas Mennel mentions in her article.

Nejat has been attempting to figure out who he is and where he came from. On his return "home," he desperately awaits a reunion with his father, who is out on the ocean, fishing. This is where the film ends: Nejat sitting on the beach looking across the ocean to the other side. One could interpret the ending as Nejat sitting between point A and point B in his journey, thus *within* the great divide, because he is not there yet, he has not crossed the ocean to be with his father. However, a different reading of the ending is possible as well.

The Broken Circle

I mentioned earlier that Nejat's journey is presented as a narrative that starts where his travels eventually end, or so it seems, presenting life as an apparent circle. Yet this is not quite the case, as the "circle of life" within the film is only mimicking a circle. It is, in fact, a false circle, and it is emblematic of the other main characters' inner journeys as well, supporting Homi Bhabha's description of the lives of exiles that lack endings and beginnings, for example, the endless ocean, the "beyond" with the promise of a new beginning. A future, to which the film has been alluding, is a deception. There is no "beyond," or if there is, it consists of either a new horizon or a leaving behind of the past; yet an escape from life is impossible, for Nejat "beyond" signifies spatial distance (see the many elements of a road movie in this film), promises the future, and marks progress. As Bhabha remarks in *The Location of Culture*, "Beginnings and endings may be the sustaining myths of the middle years; but in the fin de siècle, we find ourselves in the moment of transit where space and time cross to produce complex figures of difference and identity, past and present, inside and outside, inclusion and exclusion" (Bhabha 2).

The various criss-crossings we see in the film combined with the moments in which characters cross paths—always a little bit off, just like the star-crossed lovers Romeo and Juliet—more than underline the above. In fact, the film text foregrounds exchanges, travel, and time; however, it also self-consciously dislodges chronological time in that it tells the story out of sequence. For example, at first sight, with the film starting where it ends, the fragmented, nonlinear, and intricately tangled narrative appears to mimic the linearity of a circle, except that the circle is not round. The self—that is, Nejat's self—is written while the visual text develops; floating in and out of the past, never fully in either the past or the present. Nejat is a work in progress.

Needless to say, Nejat Aksu is a complex figure, shown at both the beginning and the end of the film in front of the Black Sea as it meets the sky. Structurally, the beginning and ending of Akin's cinematic text are no longer neatly separated, but blended together. Nor are his outer and inner journeys separated; rather, his (hi)story is presented as an outer journey mirroring his inner journey. Because the film text only pretends to have a beginning and an end it gives the impression of a circular narrative, the end following the beginning in chronological order and both "ends" meeting, framing Nejat's story. This fake setup is soon revealed when we as viewers find out that the film tells Nejat's and others' stories out of sequence, outside of the ordinary concept of time. Is the circular narrative built on linear time a foreign concept within the exile experience? It seems so, for film content and film structure complement each other, supporting Homi Bhabha's description of the life of an exile that lacks an ending and a beginning, and supporting Kristeva's notion of the concept of "woman's time," which registers events/fact/reality not in chronological order but in the order of important events.

It is thus not surprising that Fatih Akin has chosen to incorporate elements of the road movie in his film, for there is a challenge to be met just as in the *Bildungsroman*: the journey continues endlessly. In other words, the challenge never ends and life continues: a never-ending story. The direct translation of the German film title, we recall, is *On the Other Side*; yet Fatih Akin had originally settled for *On the Other Side of Life (Auf der anderen Seite des Lebens)*.[8] Knowing what we know now, his original title would have fit as well: not only would it have added to the death motif that structures Akin's film; it would also have highlighted the contrast between death and life, the "border" between locale A and locale B. However, given that this border is a deception, that the circle is not round, and that the narrative is nonlinear, Akin's final title is well chosen, for it shows

that Nejat, the eternal foreigner, is just part of this *in between*, alienated in life, alienated for life. He is neither completely Turkish nor
German but somewhat both. His journey is the subtext for the
structure of Akin's film text. And his story (narrative) is related to
other stories (narratives), like Ayten's/Gül's, for example, erasing an
imaginary border once again.

Nejat, then, as the foreigner, has not lost the soul of the alienated,
as Theodor Adorno would say. In fact, his journey of self-discovery
points to the torment that accompanies confronting the foreign
within himself. For that is what he does by choosing to travel to the
edge of heaven. The female characters are traveling as well, but, with
the exception of Ayten/Gül, their journeys are short and devoid of the
complications of Nejat's travel.

Charlotte

Neither a *fanaticist* by Kristeva's description, nor a woman on the
run, Charlotte is a product of Germany's well-to-do (well-situated)
middle class and feels quite at home in her country. Her liberal views
concerning Germany's immigration politics, which she criticizes
within the sheltered walls of her mother's house, are not uncommon
among the more educated Germans; and she, like them, expresses
them without resorting to violence, and without even being politically motivated to undermine these politics. What we see when we
see Charlotte is a young, energetic, helpful student who is curious
about the "Other." She has just returned from a three-month trip
to India—the experience-collecting journey so many young people
with a good upbringing undertake, in the footsteps of Goethe, one
of Germany's cultural fathers, who journeyed to Italy in his younger
years—and she is eager to get to know the woman from Turkey.
Shortly after they meet, she invites Ayten/Gül into her mother's
home without knowing too much about her. By taking Ayten/Gül
under her wing, and by eventually turning her back on her university
studies and moving to Istanbul in order to secure Ayten/Gül's release
from prison, Charlotte, the young and somewhat naïve woman still
in search of herself, has found her true calling: she wants to help the
friend who, for her, represents the many "others" that Germany has
a difficult time accepting.[9] In an endearing, refreshing way, Charlotte is goal oriented, opening herself up to a complete stranger. She

thereby discovers Kristeva's "foreigner" within herself, the "other" every one of us, according to the philosopher, needs to get to know in order to welcome and appreciate the "other" among us. Charlotte often embraces "otherness" too idealistically and consequently gets herself into difficult situations, like the "white middle-class tourist" abroad, who is out of her element yet eager to help. She pays for her idealism with her life, thereby adding to the life/death motif that dominates in *The Edge of Heaven*. In many ways, she is just a tourist, not the classical figure of the *Bildungsroman* who travels with the intent to get to know herself.

Susanne, a Stranger in Her Home

In Charlotte's mother, Susanne, we see a depiction of someone who has not acknowledged the "foreignness" within herself until more than half way through the film. Jealously watching her daughter getting more and more intimate with the foreign girl in her house, the middle-class mother feels most comfortable being part of a Western liberal democracy. She is convinced that both the country Turkey and the girl Ayten will get to know freedom and liberty once Turkey joins the European Union. Susanne has not yet experienced life in Turkey, the "other side" (*die andere Seite*—the German title of Akin's film). Her emotional conversations with Ayten/Gül portray her as a liberal in the Western sense in that she is determined to enlighten the foreigner in her country about Western democratic values. With a critical eye, filmmaker Akin chooses Susanne's middle-class home, primarily the kitchen where she is preparing a cherry pie, as the locale for Ayten's/Gül's and Susanne's heated discussion about the values Ayten/Gül had been fighting for in Istanbul's underground. It is interesting to note that the kitchen is where feminist politics were made back in the 1970s.[10] A shot of a kitchen in women's films is almost always a stab at the notion that women are responsible for the cooking, and for the family's children under the auspices of a (Christian) god (*Kinder, Küche, Kirche*). That is why the kitchen became a place in which personal problems, child-rearing issues, work, and political ideas were discussed in the later films (*New German Cinema*). However, in the kitchen in *The Edge of Heaven*, a discussion is not truly happening. Instead, a disagreement between

Susanne and Ayten/Gül, consisting primarily of a yelling of slogans and stereotypes, takes place. The result is not an enlightening debate, but a heated argument without result or resolve. Might the film be asking if we have settled for so little only forty years after the Second Women's Movement? And is the superficiality that characterizes the two women in this scene Akin's depiction of how we "invite" the "other" into our home today; that is, not as a welcome guest as he or she would have been invited by the ancient Greeks many years ago?[11] As the Turkish-German filmmaker makes plain, not only is Susanne culpable of using banalities, but Ayten/Gül, too, uses terms that have become rather hollow over time: liberty and freedom. Ayten/Gül is young, and still a rebel at heart, but Susanne should know better. However, Susanne's world is still small; a confrontation with new ideas and values, which would entail a rethinking of her own, has not taken place yet.

The kitchen as center of a home frequently represents the home, which can be defined as a "place, region, or state to which one properly belongs, on which one's affections centre, or where one finds refuge, rest, or satisfaction" (*Oxford English Dictionary*, qtd. in Naficy 68). Furthermore, as Naficy asserts, "'home' may be taken away or shrivel into an empty shell" (ibid.).

The latter is happening to Susanne after the arrival of Ayten/Gül, after the loss of her mother role, and definitely after the death of her daughter. Although her home is not literally being taken away, it is no longer the place that it was before Ayten/Gül appears, at least it seems to have changed. With Ayten's/Gül's arrival, Susanne appears to lead an existence in the shadow of two young women who come and go as they please and take what they need—primarily food. Susanne is amazed at how they take for granted the shelter and provisions her house—she—provides. As Charlotte and Ayten/Gül come home from a party, intoxicated and loud, she watches from behind a curtain in an upstairs bedroom: jealous, perhaps, of the "woman from nowhere" who is invading her home, taking her daughter away, and causing Susanne to be superfluous. For all we know she herself feels estranged in her own house, where she quietly reads the newspaper, stretched out on her couch, then is suddenly interrupted by the loud laughter and presence of the young women. Her privacy is disrupted; her private life, her soul, unbalanced, and her mother role diminished. When she bakes a pie in the kitchen—the heart of her home—we wonder, for whom may it be? There seems to be no one to share it with. Needless to say, her home is on its way to becoming an empty shell. Susanne finds herself no longer at its center but at its periphery, estranged: a stranger in her own house.

Susanne's Journey

Yet things change as Susanne steps onto the "other side": Istanbul. It is, unfortunately, only after the death of her daughter that she decides to travel and to take control of her own life by picking up the pieces and taking action. As happens frequently—and we see it with Gül in the book *Demircinin Kizi*—pain, here caused by her daughter's wrongful death (a result of a child's firing off of Ayten's/Gül's gun), helps her confront the unknown and to open herself up to the foreign within herself.

After her daughter's death, Susanne discovers much about Charlotte and also about herself. By sleeping in Charlotte's room, smelling her clothes packed away in boxes, frequenting the German bookstore, and reading her diaries, she sees for the first time what type of a human being her daughter really was: a caring person, standing up for those who were less fortunate than she. A particular passage in Charlotte's diary catches her attention, for it opens her eyes. Charlotte writes about herself discovering the world, cutting the umbilical cord to shelter, warmth, and the familiar: "These steps, my steps, I would like to take them powerfully . . . Mom does not understand."[12] Susanne reads that she herself, in Charlotte's eyes, went the same way: "[Mother] took the same path as I. Maybe it is that? She sees herself in me."[13] What we can take away from these scenes is that Charlotte presents part of the unknown, the foreign, which Susanne has to discover and understand before she can find herself. And Charlotte opens Susanne's eyes by telling her mother why she may be dissatisfied with her daughter's action, why she wants her to follow a different path in life. It is because Charlotte's action is what Susanne wants for herself, but not for her daughter. Unfortunately, discovering Charlotte and herself did not happen until after she had a chance to speak with her daughter. Time has not been on her side, as is frequently the case in this film, in which things are always a "little bit off."

Nevertheless, Susanne becomes a "mother" to Nejat. She offers him an insight that only a parent can give, and, in this particular circumstance, only someone who has accepted the "other" and recognized the "other" within herself. In one of the most important scenes in the film, Nejat and Susanne look out the window in Nejat's apartment in Istanbul and see an Iman calling for prayer. It is the Festival of Sacrifice, *Kurban Bayrami*, during which Abraham's willingness to sacrifice his son as a demonstration of loyalty to God (Allah) is celebrated. In a close-up shot of the older Susanne and the younger Nejat in front of a window through which we can see men answering the call to prayer, Susanne asks Nejat about his relationship with his father.

Nejat tells her that the story of Abraham offering his son to God scared him, but his father said that to save his son he (Ali) would make even God his enemy. It is at this point that Nejat decides to leave Istanbul for the Black Sea to look for his father. Intuitively or knowingly, Susanne, it appears, has given Nejat the insight he needed to take his next, "final" journey, the one that will bring him closer to his father and to peace with himself. Through this action, Susanne, who has just lost a daughter, shows us that she is capable of understanding and sincerely helping Nejat. Having stepped outside the borders of her home, she has thus come a long way. During her journey, she crossed outer and inner borders that would have been insurmountable before; moreover, her emotional pain, resulting from her daughter's death, catapulted her into accepting and even adopting the "other": Ayten/Gül, Istanbul, Nejat. From her sheltered, secluded, private life at home in Germany, Susanne has sprung out into the world and into action; after losing a daughter, she has saved "a son."

Ali

In a similar vein, Ali has adopted the "Other" as well. And like Susanne, he too arrives in Istanbul from Germany, and at the same time. The film connects the plight/awakening of both parents by filming the two side by side at the passport control at the airport; furthermore, the film makes use of a crosscut from Susanne's reading of her daughter's diary to Ali's reading of the book *Die Tochter des Schmieds*, in order to, again as I would argue, underline their similar journeys. Ali, older and wiser looking, puts down the book and slowly shakes his head. He has tears in his eyes as he looks into the distance, across the ocean (the other side?). He too realizes what his son had tried to tell him: "You left me, I caused you pain, I love you." Kazim Koyuncu's message in his song "Ben Seni Sevdigimi," which we hear early on in the film, rings true.

Female Souls Transitioning and Arriving

In conclusion, in this chapter I have attempted to describe the various exilic journeys the main characters in *The Edge of Heaven* engage in on their way to self-discovery. Departing from death/pain, their travels take them to new heights both inwardly and outwardly. Foreigners to others and to themselves, they live in limbo, outside the mythical circle of life, as Nejat's traveling narratives make clear. In some exile literature, the notion of *diaspora* is evoked, which is a fitting term to describe the *feeling of exile*. It is helpful to turn to the German word for diaspora, *Zerstreuung*, as it has a double meaning; on the one hand it means scatteredness and on the other distraction (Peters 17). For example, while A and B (origin and geographic destination) characterize the inner makeup of the characters as well as the spatial and temporal configurations of the film text, they, it follows, also invoke the same type of *Zerstreuung* within the audience of the film who experience a kind of exile from their authentic center. As *The Edge of Heaven* enters and exits the souls of others, it asks us to do the same. Furthermore, through its criss-crossings and other spatial and temporal markers, it heightens the very space of transit-as-transition. What it still lacks and what is not atypical for many films, including the road movies from which Akin borrows, is a foregrounding of the *female* traveling experience. The feminist critic Giuliana Bruno states, "We have not yet completed the task of expanding feminist horizons in the arena of traveling cultures" (Bruno 85). Bruno asks us to look at feminist film theory with a geographer's eyes in order to expose how travel in (film) space may map sexual difference. It could help us understand "sexual difference in terms of space—as a geography of negotiated terrains" (ibid.).

Although the female traveling experience is not the main focus in Fatih Akin's film, it is nevertheless not degraded to the point of being hidden, far from it. Too many criss-crossings involving female characters (Yeter, Ayten/Gül) take place, and the intertextual connection between the written word and the visual text hinges on a woman (Gül). And while it is true that, historically, road movies associate the value of the road with the male gender, today's road movies have expanded the role of women. In classics like *Thelma and Louise* and *Bandits*,[14] women experience being more alive and free than in their previous experiences under male domination at home; it is just that along the way, they took a wrong turn. In *The Edge of Heaven*, which is not a road movie per se but a hybrid film that includes, among others, elements of the road movie, women who take a wrong turn die or are reborn before they metamorphose into lawful guests in a foreign country. Such is the case with Ayten/Gül who carries an illegal weapon while working on behalf of a terrorist organization, and who eventually succumbs to the laws of her country and breaks contact with her former gang leaders (all women). The women on the right road—Ayten/Gül and Susanne—are more alive than ever. Together, with their memory of Charlotte, and their aim to work toward the goals Charlotte set for herself, the pair has found a new home in the city of Istanbul. Unlike the foreigner per se, Nejat, whose travels will never end, the two finally arrive. Their souls are either at the end of their transit stage or at a new beginning, where they find peace, harmony, and perhaps even the happiness denied the main character in this film: the endless male traveler who never arrives.

Notes

1. Part of this chapter is forthcoming in the *International Journal for the Humanities* in an article titled "Home, Alienhood and Transcience in Stephen Frears' *Dirty Pretty Things* and Fatih Akin's *The Edge of Heaven*" (2012).
2. http://www.victorian.web.org/genre/hader1.html.
3. In response to a labor shortage caused by economic recovery shortly after World War II, Germany signed a series of bilateral recruitment agreements with Italy (1955), Spain and Greece (1960s), Turkey (1961), Portugal (1964), and Yugoslavia (1968). See http://www/migration information.org/Profiles/display.cfm?ID=235, June 27, 2010.

4. During an intimate moment, Ayten tells Charlotte, her girlfriend, that her real name is Gül, but Ayten is the name she uses in her falsified papers.
5. Kristeva points out that "the foreigner lives within us: he is the hidden face of our identity, the space that wrecks our abode, the time in which understanding and affinity founder. By recognizing him within ourselves, we are spared detecting him in himself" (Kristeva 1).
6. "Gül" translates into "rose" in English.
7. Martens, quoted in Mennel 16.
8. See the interview with Fatih Akin in the German release of the DVD *Auf der Anderen Seite*, in which he discusses his choosing of the title for this film.
9. According to a report by the U.N., even a year after Akin's movie was released, the Federal Republic of Germany has still not fulfilled the Geneva Convention's criteria against all types of racism. A U.N. committee (CERD) found an increase in racist-related crimes in Germany, in particular against Muslims, Sinti and Roma (gypsies), Jews, and refugees from Africa. Furthermore, the committee stated that non-German women who are victims of a crime receive, generally speaking, less money in retribution than German women; and that racist language is still prevalent in some of the paperwork migrants have to complete upon entering the Federal Republic. Moreover, even though of all Germans one-fifth have migrant backgrounds, and 8 percent are foreigners (those without a German passport), the German government's report on antiracist measurements lacks detailed statistics regarding the ethnic makeup of all inhabitants of Germany. Last but not least, the terms *racism* and *racist discrimination* are not even defined in Germany's constitution, and those who commit racially motivated crimes do not receive harsher penalties than do those who commit crimes that are not racially motivated. See Web. 29 June (2010). <http://www.taz.de/1/politik/deutschland/artikel/1/deutsche-auslaender-diskriminiert/>
10. The Second German Women's Movement grew out of the German Student Movement. Many filmmakers (like Helma Sanders-Brahms and Helke Sander among others) were politically active in establishing kindergartens for single working mothers like themselves, in working on behalf of underpaid women working in the film industry, and through their representation in Students for a Democratic Society—a student political organization dominated by men. As a filmmaker well versed in German film history, Akin was most likely aware of

the kitchen as the center of many of the German women's films from the 1960s, 1970s, and 1980s, which played with the concept "Kinder, Kirche, Küche"—children, church, kitchen—known as KKK in history books, and stressing the three pillars that made a good wife and mother in the period following World War II.

11. Tolerance toward the "other" was the norm. For Plato, the foreigner "shall depart as a friend, taking leave of friends, and be honored by them with gifts and suitable tributes of respect" (Kristeva 56).

12. "Diese Schritte, meine Schritte, möchte ich kraftvoll gehen . . . Mama versteht das nicht" (my translation).

13. "[S]ie ging dabei die gleichen Wege wie ich. Vielleicht ist es das? Sie sieht sich selbst in mir" (my translation).

14. Ridley Scott, *Thelma and Louise* (USA, 1991), and Katja von Garnier, *Bandits* (Germany, 1997).

Works Cited

Baumann, Zygmunt. "Assimilation into Exile: The Jew as a Polish Writer." *Poetics Today* 17.4 (Winter 1996): 1. Print.

Bhabha, Homi. *The Location of Culture.* London: Routledge, 1994. Print.

"Bildungsroman." <http://www.victorian.web.org/genre/hader1.html>. Web. July 2, 2011.

Bruno, Giuliana. *Atlas of Emotion: Journeys in Art, Architecture, and Film.* London: Verso, 2002. Print.

Kristeva, Julia. *The Portable Kristeva.* New York: Columbia UP, 1997. Print.

———. *Strangers to Ourselves.* New York: Columbia UP, 1991. Print.

Martens, Helge. "Goethe und der Basaltstreit." 11. *Sitzung der Humboldt-Gesellschaft* 13.6 (1995): 1–7. Web. <http://www.humboldtgesellschaft.de/druck.php?name=goethe>. June 6, 2011.

Mennel, Barbara. "Criss-Crossing in Space and Time: Fatih Akin's *The Edge of Heaven (2007)." Transit: A Journal of Travel, Migration and Multiculturalism in the German-speaking World* 5.1 (2010). Web. June 15, 2011. <http://german.berkeley.edu/transit/>.

Naficy, Hamid. *An Accented Cinema: Accented and Diasporic Filmmaking.* Princeton: Princeton UP, 2001. Print.

Oezcan, Veysel. "Germany Immigration in Transition." <http://www.migrationinformation.org/Profiles/display.cfm?ID=235>. Web. June 27, 2010.

Özdogan, Selim. *Die Tochter des Schmieds.* Berlin: Aufbau, 2007.

Peters, John Durham. "Exile, Nomadism, Diaspora." *Home, Exile, Homeland: Film, Media, and the Politics of Place.* Ed. Hamid Naficy. New York: Routledge. 17–41. Print.

Roberson, Susan L. *Defining Travel: Diverse Visions.* Jackson: Mississippi UP, 2002. Print.

Said, Edward. "Intellectual Exile: Expatriates and Marginals." *Grand Street* 12.3 (1993): 112. Print.

7

Female Transnational Migrations and Diasporas in European "Immigration Cinema"

Isolina Ballesteros

Overview

*I*mmigration films made by women give their subjects a voice that is *often at odds with much of the general assumptions on female immigration.* Flores de otro mundo (Flowers from Another World*) by Icíar Bollaín (1999);* Inch'Allah dimanche (God Willing, It's Sunday*) by Yamina Benguigui (2001);* Extranjeras (Female Foreigners*) by Helena Taberna (2002); and* Bhaji on the Beach *(1993) by Gurinder Chadha emphasize the essential role of female communities for adaptation and interracial coexistence and reflect on cultural and religious aspects that affect and frequently prevent or delay women's full integration in the adopted country. Concentrating on women immigrants' interaction with diasporic and adapted communities, these films ignore the widespread yet incomplete media sensationalist discourses on female migration and present alternatives to immigration films that opt for stories about women caught in no-exit situations and that are constructed in terms of exploitation, seclusion, and isolation. The films show a tendency found within immigration films made by women: a common desire to undo female migrants' invisibility. They focus on the* *processes of family reunion and integration of migrant women within the workforce and highlight their contribution to the preservation of traditions as well as the creation of sociality and solidarity networks.*

Since the early 1990s, the inexorable trend of global transnational migrations and the moral and social dilemmas linked to them have captured the interest of intellectuals, activists, and artists, permeating diverse areas of the cultural arena and gradually penetrating collective awareness. An increasing number of recent European films focus explicitly on the current phenomena of immigration and xenophobia and try to provide alternatives to the partial coverage made available by the media, which typically limits itself to sensationalist accounts. In a previous essay I coined the term *immigration cinema* to describe this new genre, one that contains a varied corpus of films representing contemporary immigration— and the ramifications of racism and xenophobia—as well as the heterogeneous immigrant subject. I defined "immigration cinema" as a subcategory of "world cinema" and "third cinema," treated in relation to notions such as hybridity, transculturation, border crossing, transnationalism, and translation. As Ella Shohat acknowledges, in diasporic and post-Third-Worldist films, "the boundaries between the personal and communal, like the generic boundaries between documentary and fiction, the biographic and the ethnographic, are constantly blurred. These films function as a collective memory of colonial violence and postcolonial displacement" (Shohat 74). Along the same lines, my conception of "immigration cinema" resists categorization within Film Studies' established and canonical categories of production and reception, which are based on notions of authorship or national identity. The unmappable and hybrid condition of immigration cinema results also from its free combination and deliberate blurring of filmic conventions pertaining to two or more genres. These films' approaches and methods ensue from their filmmakers' understanding of cinema as a cultural, ideological, and ethical apparatus that represents the intersection of race, gender, sexuality, and class, and seeks communal awareness.[1]

Within the broad context of responses to the global phenomenon of migratory movements, it remains a poignant fact that political as

well as media discourses consistently deny or minimize female protagonism (Nash 21), reducing the panoply of migrant women's roles
and contributions to domesticity and depicting them as dependent,
economically passive subjects, often contextualized solely in terms
of family reunification, domestic service, and sexual work (26). To
counteract that lack, feminist sociologists have denounced since
the 1980s the general lack of awareness regarding female migration
in spite of the considerable amount of related studies. To this end,
they have shown that existing literature has a male bias insofar as it
ignores the contribution of immigrant women to the development
of a future workforce (Kofman 287), therefore having little impact
on policymakers and the media (Morokvasic 899). By analyzing
legislation and immigration policies, these sociologists have also
pointed out that the state contributes to the construction of a labor
market segmented along gender lines, sustaining female dependency
in conformity to the model of the nuclear family (Kofman 279; Solé
and Parella 68), and allowing for subcontracting networks in areas
traditionally considered as feminine. In Western countries where the
recruitment of overseas labor migrants is organized by the state and
laws give total control to employers, female immigrants maintain
the global sweatshop economy, the garment industry's workforce,
and the domestic service industry (usually involving child care and
housekeeping) (Raijman, Schammah-Gesser, and Kemp 733).[2]

A variety of studies have also documented that because women
have limited access to and representation within mass media, their
opinions do not count as much or are deemed irrelevant (Dijk 39).
In order to bridge that gap, many European female (and some male)
filmmakers have engaged the issue of immigration by giving voice
to the subaltern, counteracting the female immigrant's social invisibility and media indifference and generating "strategies of positive
self-representation" (40). Their films attempt to correct the reduc-
tionist framework used to contemplate female migratory patterns,
providing feminist approaches that emphasize agency in female
migrants and call attention to the roles they play in maintaining
transnational economic networks. Moreover, women filmmakers
find diverse and heterogeneous ways of portraying the relationship between the local and the migrant Other, highlighting the

importance of family reunion and the role of women's solidarity in the creation and perpetuation of diasporas.

In European countries with a long tradition of immigration and established diasporas, such as the United Kingdom, France, and Germany, second-generation immigrants have joined European filmmakers in their mission to represent female migrants' agency, mostly from a personal perspective. They often conceive of their films as autobiographical projects that provide a way to understand their own hybrid identities, and the challenges of living in-between. They emphasize the role of mothers and grandmothers in laying the ground for the next generation, and their films often function as homage to them. As documented by Meenakshi Thapan, women figure out "strategies to deal with the sense of dislocation," and "they return to the past staged metaphorically and narratologically through films and videos . . . songs and poems" (30). Second-generation immigrant's films function as a reenactment of their immigrant past, enacting nostalgia for the ancestral homeland and serving as a way to deal with the sense of dislocation to which Thapan refers.

To illustrate the aforementioned aspects, I have selected four recent European immigration films made by women: *Bhaji on the Beach* (1993) by Gurinder Chadha; *Flores de otro mundo/Flowers from Another World* (1999) by Icíar Bollaín; *Inch'Allah dimanche/ Good Willing, It's Sunday* (2001) by Yamina Benguigui; and *Extranjeras/Female Foreigners* (2002) by Helena Taberna. I analyze these films as precise examples of a tendency found within immigration films made by women, which show a common desire to undo female migrants' invisibility, focusing on the processes of family reunion and integration of migrant women within the workforce and highlighting their contribution to the preservation of traditions as well as to the creation of networks of sociality and solidarity. By concentrating on women immigrants' interaction with diasporic and adopted communities, these four films ignore widespread yet incomplete media sensationalist discourses on female migration and present alternatives to immigration films that opt for stories about women caught in no-exit situations and that are constructed in terms of exploitation, seclusion, and isolation.[3]

Home, Family Reunion, and the Redefinition
of Diasporic Identities

Inch'Allah dimanche was conceived by Yamina Benguigui (born and raised in France to Algerian parents) as a personal project that pays homage to her own mother, a work of memory that captures the experiences of the first wave of Algerian female immigrants to France. It tells the story of Zouina who arrives in France with her three children following the 1974 family reunion law that allowed Algerian women to rejoin their husbands working in the country. With a tragicomic tone, Benguigui documents the hardships Zouina has to suffer in order to adapt to the new foreign society and to finally liberate herself from the limitations imposed on women within her native culture, which are strongly embodied by the matriarch of the family, the grotesque, monsterlike mother-in-law, Aïcha.

Benguigui locates her character at the intersection of, and in the process of transition and negotiation between, the oppressive traditions imposed by her cultural heritage and the simultaneous liberties and oppressive preconceptions about Muslim foreigners that are prevalent in France. As sociologists have noted, women migrants are generally more committed than men to keeping their links with their countries of origin (Zontini 110). This commitment results sometimes from the need to deal with the sense of dislocation through the reenactment of traditional roles and re-creation of the homeland, "as a strategic move to resist the subordinate, inferior and demeaning definitions of their race and class position in the host country" (Thapan 31). *Inch'Allah* illustrates the difficulty women have in challenging patriarchal authority, especially when patriarchy is sustained and solidified through matriarchy in their native culture, but also shows the extent to which immigrant communities preserve and value their traditions and cultural practices in order to survive in a hostile society that can only see them as strangers. Most important, it highlights the dual role women play in diasporas as both keepers of traditions from the old country and organizers of spaces of community and socialization in the new society, acting as the fundamental link between the two worlds.

The film's action is driven by Zouina's desperate need to connect to her roots and keep her culture's traditions through the communal celebration of Eid—a large family holiday in Algeria with the custom of offering cakes to friends and family in memory of a deceased family member, and for whom a sheep must also be sacrificed. In order to celebrate Eid, every Sunday, while her husband and mother-in-law search for the sacrificial sheep, Zouina secretly leaves her home accompanied by her three children and goes through a myriad of arduous adventures in search of an Algerian family with whom to share the celebration. The resolution of the character (as well as the meaning of the film's title) involves a paradox: Zouina's insistence on preserving a tradition and socializing with other Algerians facilitates her liberation and integration into French society. Indeed, her agency contradicts the stereotype of immigrant women as passive women dependent on their husbands, and a new liberated and hybrid identity ensues from her willingness to reach out to and make alliances with other women. Her attempts to establish a connection with Malika,[4] the mother of the only other Algerian family in town, fail in the end: upon seeing Zouina's courage and willingness to rebel against patriarchal impositions, Malika breaks her culture's hospitality rules and rejects her in an act that shows her self-imposed resignation to patriarchal oppression. While Zouina screams, cries, and breaks a window-glass with her hand in an attempt to change Malika's mind, a cut to Malika cloistered inside the house shows her in slow motion, unresponsive to Zouina's plight but emotionally devastated by her determination. Taken together, Zouina's melodramatic reaction to Malika's rejection and Malika's self-protective lack of solidarity emphasize the gap between the two women, prompt spectatorial empathy toward both of them, and produce a catharsis leading to Zouina's happy, yet implausible, liberation at the end of the film. With the help of a friendly bus driver from the neighborhood, Zouina returns home with her injured hand bandaged with her headscarf,[5] only to find her family and neighbors anxiously waiting for her. Her escapade has been discovered, but her husband, instead of beating her or yelling at her as he did in earlier scenes, looks her in the eye for the first time, accepts her willingness to take the children to school from then on, and confronts his mother's alienating authority.

Malika and Aïcha, the castrating mother-in-law, function as guarantors of the Algerian tradition of feminine subservience

(Fauvel 152) and as counterparts to Zouina's desire to integrate into France and benefit from the liberties enjoyed by French women. As Maryse Fauvel has shown in her lucid analysis of the film, the contrast between these women's and Zouina's transition from imprisonment to liberation is visually translated through the fluctuation between closed/open spaces and subjective/objective shots (149). Close-ups and medium shots situate Zouina inside the closed spaces of the house or the interior garden and highlight her suffocation and feelings of imprisonment. She is typically framed by windows and doorways that represent passages to the outside world and symbolize her desire to reach beyond the confines of the domestic space and chores. On her Sunday escapades, both long shots and extremely long shots depict Zouina and her children lost in the middle of an unknown and vast landscape. Through them, Benguigui emphasizes the family's displacement and vulnerability but also the freedom of movement they lack inside the house.

Her character is defined by her silence in the domestic realm, which is dominated by her mother-in-law's loud voice accusing her of being a bad wife and mother, insulting and cursing her, as well as by her verbal skillfulness in the public sphere, whether shopping for groceries in the neighborhood or talking to other women in her pursuit of a community. Although voiceless and motionless inside the house, Zouina is granted the gaze—she is consistently framed peering through the window and observing neighbors—by which she establishes a platonic relationship with the bus driver based on mutual visual curiosity. In violent scenes presented in extreme opposition to her otherwise silent and abiding demeanor, Zouina's agency is progressively constructed through subtle daily transgressions: opening the door to unknown people; listening to a daily radio program addressed to women; applying and hiding the makeup that Nicole, her friendly French neighbor, has given her; neglecting her prayers; asking for her children's complicity in her Sunday excursions; and furiously rebelling against Nicole's hostility and Malika's stolid reaction. The mobility and verbal dexterity Zouina's character exhibits on Sundays and in the last scenes of the film illustrates the double and even plural identifications (cultural, linguistic, ethnic, national) that diasporic subjects experience and that constitute hybrid forms of identity (Braziel and Mannur 5). As Thapan points out, self and home can be "experienced in movement" (29) and "the immigrant woman thus reconstructs different aspects of her life and conceives of home and nation not in terms of either past or present but through the combination of the categories of the native as well as host society. Identities are constructed in the space between past and present, the two representing a continuum rather than separate worlds" (Thapan 55). In that sense, Zouina's desire to connect to her roots does not imply rejection of the commodities available to women in France nor of the friendship that French individuals offer her.

The film's actions are also driven by the fierce yet comedic confrontations between the female (Algerian and French) homemakers taking place in the adjacent backyards. The French next-door neighbors, Mr. and Mrs. Donze, are caricatures of the French nation's panic in the face of Otherness as well as agents of the film's comic relief. Reminiscent of Ben Jelloun's text, *French Hospitality: Racism and North African Immigrants*, the Donzes are disturbed by the "primitive" customs of their Algerian neighbors who among other things make coffee, spit, and play ball in the backyard. Their arrival with their different habits produces a culture shock that evidences what Jelloun has called the "threshold of tolerance": a type of peaceful, benign, racism that holds the idea that "it's impossible for different cultures and the people belonging to them to coexist peacefully" (Ben Jelloun 87). This theory concedes individuals and cultures "the right to be different as long as hierarchical relationships are preserved," and translates into a praxis that encourages the herding together of immigrants in transit centers, hostels, and insalubrious districts, therefore abhorring situations of neighborly coexistence (87–88).

In the film, the Donzes' backyard (separated from their Algerian neighbors' backyard only by a short fence) functions as a metaphor of the French nation and by extension of Fortress Europe: it has to be carefully tended and kept beautiful for the annual garden competition and its borders have to be heavily guarded to prevent the immigrant neighbors from invading and destroying it. The Donzes are willing to commit acts of violence in order to "protect" their property from invasion: Mrs. Donze "kills a ball" that accidentally rolls into her backyard, and on her turn Zouina retaliates by attacking Mrs. Donze and breaking a decorative clay rooster—the national symbol of France. Immigrants and their children are likened by nationals to "weeds that invade the whole garden, that you have to pull up" (Ben Jalloun 94). When Zouina acknowledges that she is growing mint in her backyard, Mrs. Douze frets that this "foreign weed" will spread quickly and contaminate her very French garden, then discovers, upon looking up the word in the plants encyclopedia, that mint is a native French herb.

The tragicomic tone achieved by these symbolic confrontations becomes ironic as Benguigui creates parallel scenes in the two households in which the two women, Algerian and French, conduct the same domestic chores and listen to the same radio programs. Through the mirroring of these women's private spheres and endeavors, Benguigui erodes the dichotomic representation of the two households in terms of invaders/invaded and creates the notion of the need for solidarity and communication between women who share the same experiences and have the same interests. The animosity developed between the two women is also compensated for by the friendship and support offered to Zouina by her other neighbor Nicole and by the widow of a French general who died in Algeria during colonial times, whom she met while looking for Malika.[6] The links Zouina creates with these French women pave the road to her acceptance of and integration into the new society and create a "continuum between the two worlds."

Flores de otro mundo is not a film about family reunion in the traditional sense but about family repopulation, interracial relations, and miscegenation in Spain. The film documents the arrival of three women (one Spaniard and two immigrants) at the remote Castilian village of Santa Eulalia as part of a repopulation project, and their interactions with the rural community during the following year.[7] The two immigrants, Patricia and Milady, are from the Caribbean. Patricia, a single mother of two from the Dominican Republic, has lived in Spain for four years and is looking for familial stability for her children and herself. She marries Damián, a local farmer who lives with his widowed mother and who offers her respect, affection, and security. Milady is a twenty-year-old Cuban who arrives in the village invited by Carmelo, a local contractor and former lover of hers whom she met during one of his touristic visits to the island. Milady left Cuba looking for new horizons, mobility, and economic comfort; but uninformed about what kind of place Santa Eulalia is, she does not easily adapt to the village's customs and expectations and ends up leaving, just as Carmelo turns progressively more possessive and violent.

Icíar Bollaín delves into some of the same topics that Benguigui explores in her film, topics such as migrant women's survival in a hostile society aided by feminine solidarity yet hindered by native women who thwart their integration efforts. Other topics include use of the mother-in-law character as an emblem and defender of the native Nation from contamination; the simultaneity of displacement and movement as aspects consubstantial to the immigrants' characterization; the immigrant's final liberation from both patriarchal domestic abuse and matriarchal authority; and the construction of domestic stability as a legitimate option for both securing citizenship for immigrants and preventing the disappearance of Spanish rural communities.

Bollaín starts by denouncing the homogenizing and eroticizing processes women migrants are submitted to, which are presented as consubstantial to racism. She mocks old villagers for their inability to distinguish between the "Dominican" and "the Cuban" when Milady arrives at the village, and for referring to the women only as men's possessions: "Damián's woman" and "Carmelo's woman." She also exposes the villagers' stereotyped preconceptions about black Caribbean women, which include exoticism, sexual prowess, promiscuity, and opportunism ("they only come to obtain work papers"). To contradict this homogenizing tendency, the film emphasizes, on the one hand, the differences between the immigrant women in terms of their age, national identity, profession, independence, exposure and commitment to the rural world, and willingness to assimilate. On the other hand, Bollaín's film emphasizes the commonalities they share with the women in the Spanish village. She creates for each character a different outcome in order to challenge the suspicion that they came just for work papers: Patricia assumes the traditional domestic roles expected by the community and adapts to the authoritarian regime of the mother-in-law, whereas Milady frees herself from Carmelo's possessive and violent attitude and leaves the village in spite of her undocumented status. Both women have to fight the village's hostility toward their Otherness. Patricia, like Zouina in *Inch'Allah*, has to negotiate every inch of her domestic space with her mother-in-law, Gregoria, a castrating mother who perpetuates patriarchy, much like Aïcha in *Inch'Allah*. Gregoria perceives the exotic foreigner as a threat to her sovereignty in the house, which figuratively represents the Spanish nation as a fortress being invaded by aliens. Milady's freedom and desire to know the world and move independently are violently repressed by Carmelo; her assimilation is equated to "taming," and it requires adaptation to domestic roles and spaces. Like Zouina, Milady is subjected to physical violence and restricted to the house as a consequence of her transgressions, but in the end, she refuses to be domesticated and recovers her freedom. Her character is consistently visualized in transit, defined in terms of mobility, and located in the public rather than domestic sphere.

In the film's happy outcome, Patricia's self-determination and willingness to adapt pay off, and her mother-in-law realizes that Patricia is not taking advantage of her son and that she loves him for the same reasons she herself loved her late husband. In a scene at the cemetery in which both women tend to the tomb of Gregoria's husband, they discover that what unites them is more important than what separates them. As the filmmaker has declared in interviews, her fundamental goal is to emphasize the positive aspects of miscegenation over conflicts, and to foster in the film's viewers an appreciation for the culture immigrants bring with them: the music, the color, and above all the solidarity between women.[8] The aforementioned scene at the cemetery—along with the numerous scenes that show Patricia and Milady, and Patricia and her Dominican aunt and friend, socializing and strengthening their bonds of affection and support through their shared foreignness—capture the filmmaker's belief that the adaptation of migrant women to a foreign culture is facilitated by the creation of and participation in female networks of sociality and solidarity. These networks often function along gender lines that are capable of dissolving the boundaries imposed by race, tradition, and national identity, as well as of forcing the "collapse of the opposition us versus strangers" (Bauman 68).

Domestic Service, Female Networks of Sociality, and Solidarity

A significant common element found in immigration films made by women is their inclination to portray immigrant women in traditional domestic roles or contributing to the workforce in domestic service areas. On the one hand, this trend acknowledges that domestic service does indeed provide an impetus for independent female migration. Increasingly, women in developed countries are joining the public workforce and relying on domestic help in order to successfully manage their professional and parental responsibilities. Besides representing this basic reality, these films do not simply show that demand for domestic labor provides immigrants with the resources and networks of sociality through which they can better adapt to adopted societies. They also show that in many instances the immigrants' public profile also stems from the so-called private sphere. Women inhabit the social space of the ghetto or neighborhood in a much more interactive way than do men through the formation of fixed habits, daily interactions, and banal conversations with neighbors in stores, public squares, playgrounds, and other public spaces. Their activities in the public space are a continuation of their activities in the private, domestic space, or the "feminine space" (Tello i Robira 93).

Asun García Armand's research on the public roles of female immigrants in the neighborhood of El Raval in Barcelona can offer insight into situations in other Western European countries as well as elucidate the construction of a "feminine space" in women's immigration films. In her view, because of the multiplicity of "domestic" activities, which women have to assume in the neighborhood following traditional gender-role configurations, women tend to have a broader and more global vision of their environment than their male counterparts. Mainly responsible for the family's functioning, they are more visible in the neighborhood. They learn codes and symbols sooner than men do; therefore they can more quickly become potential interpreters and transmitters of those rules and codes of behavior in ways that may facilitate the family's evolution in the new environment. Traditional gender roles, generally associated with subordination and dependency, can provide a crucial source of agency as women use their roles of spouse and mother strategically. They also become agents of new identities by highlighting the similarities between their female functions and those of their autochthonous female neighbors (García Armand 135–36).

Extranjeras, Taberna's film, is in many ways a paradigmatic production within the immigration genre. Based on her interviews with female immigrants representative of the larger immigrant communities in Madrid, it is the first Spanish film to use the documentary format to give absolute protagonism to women and to follow the aforementioned "feminine" patterns of sociality and adaptation. The film contributes to Madrid's new image as a globalized and cosmopolitan city in which a conglomerate of international cultures coexists (Taberna and Costa Villaverde 37; Camí-Vela, "Entrevista" 49). In this sense, the film is successful in demonstrating the heterogeneity of migrant groups in Spain, and of migrant women's experiences.

Taberna corrects the lack of information about female migration's protagonism in the city by interviewing a large number of women who are the main breadwinners in their households and who own and manage businesses such as telephone parlors, beauty salons, restaurants, and local grocery stores. Her film makes a conscious, feminist effort to let the subaltern speak and to establish a public dialogue with women immigrants and women's associations. It counteracts the "scarcity of feminist approaches that emphasize agency in female migrants and the roles they play in maintaining transnational networks" (Kofman 288). Taberna's approach illustrates women's social function as transmitters of ethnic culture and language (Camí-Vela, "Entrevista"). The immigrants' autobiographical narratives underscore their direct participation in maintaining the language and traditions of their countries of origin and passing them on to their children. Pagan and religious celebrations and rituals are filmed on location. For example, the film shows a Chinese New Year celebration in a public square and social and musical gatherings in parks and public areas on Sundays, as well as scenes filmed at a Buddhist Temple, an Orthodox Church, and a Mosque— and always from the women's point of view. Muslim youth defend their right to wear the hijab at school—showing Taberna's respectful position toward a very controversial issue in Europe.[9] *Extranjeras* is a visual "testimonio"[10] whose subjects come from a variety of ethnicities, social and educational backgrounds, and experiences regarding racism and discrimination.

In her already canonical article "Can the Subaltern Speak?" Gayatri Spivak (referring mostly to the Indian subaltern) concluded that the economically dispossessed cannot speak because their voice is always controlled by Western transcribers, interpreters, and mediators. Spivak suggests that attempts from the outside to ameliorate the condition of Indian subalterns by granting them collective speech invariably encounter the following two problems: (1) a logocentric assumption of cultural solidarity among a heterogeneous people and (2) a dependence upon Western intellectuals to "speak for" the subaltern condition rather than allowing them to speak for themselves. By speaking out and reclaiming a collective cultural identity, Spivak argues, subalterns will in fact reinscribe their subordinate position in society.

As a positive alternative to Spivak's reservations about the potential role of the Western intellectual to ameliorate the silencing of subaltern voices, Taberna carefully attends to the heterogeneity in the collective group of immigrants she interviews, and avoids reinforcing their subaltern position in Spanish society by hiding her "intellectual" presence from the diegesis. She omits the introductory scenes and voiceover through which documentary authors traditionally declare their ethical stance. The interviewees are introduced visually, rather than orally, in the opening scenes in a series of close-up photo shoots that emphasizes the diversity of the group in terms of age, race, and ethnicity. The interviews that follow are conducted without enunciation of specific questions, which creates a sense of closeness and spontaneity as the women talk freely and in their own terms about their different experiences, and transfers to the audience the task of inferring the questions and establishing a common discursive pattern. The filmmaker's absence from the diegesis has to be read as an aesthetic as much as an ethical statement. The apparent open nature of the questions leaves ample space for improvisation in the subjects' narrations, thus facilitating the spectators' direct contact with the foreigners without the authoritative intervention of the filmmaker. By choosing to do so, Taberna also reinforces the idea that immigration is a bilateral, dual, reciprocal process that affects not only immigrant individuals but also host individuals once they both get in contact in any given way. The closing scenes are filmed at a concert by an African group formed by two of the film's protagonists. Only then does Taberna establish the connecting link between herself and all her interviewees by appearing in the scene, inadvertently to those who do not know her, among her foreign women. This last scene provides closure to her filmic text, shows the importance of social and communal female activities for these women, and validates the role that music and traditions play in unifying peoples.[11]

The selection and montage of narrative and visual material denote restrain: they avoid situations of victimization and manipulation of the audience's emotions by limiting references to their lives previous to immigration to generalities such as dire economic situations or persecution in their countries of origin. Contrary to ethnographic documentaries that focus on the suffering of specific subjects that are very distant from the spectators' daily lives, the small stories narrated in *Extranjeras* happen in ordinary neighborhoods, and are not that different from the spectators' own reality. When asked why she did not include interviews with sex workers, Taberna replied that her primary intention was to follow the ordinary lives of women who do not make the sensationalist news and to deliberately stay away from the simplistic equation established by the media between immigration and illegal border crossing, delinquency and prostitution, and that typically reinforces the stigmatization of prostitution by highlighting sexual stereotyping and exploitation situations (Camí-Vela, "Entrevista" 52).

Taberna introduces her protagonists by locating them instead in the spaces they inhabit or in which they work, both private and public. She wants to reinforce the fact that they are high achievers who have attained a level of success in Madrid with the backing and encouragement of female networks. Feminine camaraderie and networking is reinforced in encounters in public urban spaces like parks, churches, cultural associations, beauty salons, and music concerts, and Taberna takes the camera to these places in order to highlight the urban mobility and independence of these women.

In an article they coauthored, Socorro Pérez Rincón and Asun García Armand find that the reinforcement and sharing of "culinary uses" are some of the fundamental strategies of sociality for immigrant women: gastronomy is understood and implemented as a common practice to promote the exchange of identity codes and the dismantling of stereotypes. A variety of culinary celebrations serve the purpose of transmitting elements of the immigrants' culture to the host society in the public space, which becomes a space of intercultural contact. Women have a crucial role in creating such "contact spaces" where they can return symbolically to the culture of origin and reproduce it partially in the new space. These contact spaces trigger the hybridization of tastes, alimentary habits, and festivities. "Ethnic" restaurants and stores run by immigrants become intercultural spaces that can become the first step in the acceptance of foreign practices by autochthonous neighbors (Pérez Rincón and García Armand 110–12).

Vividly illustrating the findings of this research, Taberna films a gathering of the "Cocina intercultural" (Intercultural cuisine) association and the "Jornadas culinarias" (Culinary meetings) in which immigrants from different Latin American countries get together to exchange traditional dishes. Upholding the culinary traditions of their countries of origin is shown in the film to be as important for these female communities as the preservation of other major cultural components such as language and music (María Pilar Rodríguez 41). In addition to demonstrating the communal and social function of cooking in these groups, Taberna films many of her subjects inside their kitchens and interviews them while they prepare lunch or dinner. Cooking at home for family, friends, and neighbors is often transferred to the opening of their own businesses, the ethnic restaurants or catering services that become "contact spaces" for immigrants and natives alike. Telephone parlors, fundamental spaces of international communication for immigrants, are also managed by Ecuadorian women, and a delivery hub run by Polish women operates as an essential source for exchanging native newspapers and sending and receiving parcels from home. Though Taberna never shows these immigrant women interacting with Spanish women, their businesses are spaces of ethnic cultural preservation central to the immigrant's diaspora and provide the neighborhood with a space for social interaction that ultimately facilitates communication and mediation between natives and immigrants.

Immigrant Associations and Female Networking

Female networking fosters a sense of community and belonging, but it also provides very concrete services to immigrants in their process of integration into the host society. *Bhaji on the Beach*, Gurinder Chadha's feature directorial debut, follows a group of related South Asian women during a day trip to Blackpool (a traditionally white, working-class seaside resort), organized by Simi, who is the coordinator of the Saheli Asian Women's Center, an association created to provide both support and entertainment to South Asian women immigrants in their integration into British society. In all her films Chadha explores many of the dilemmas affecting South Asian women, like herself, born and living in a multicultural and hybrid United Kingdom, especially "the tension between the immigrants' loyalty to their cultural and religious traditions and their simultaneous rebellion against those norms, which inevitably arises during their progressive assimilation" (Ballesteros "Immigration Cinema" 195).[12]

Bhaji on the Beach examines the generational gap between three generations of South Asian women regarding their process of assimilation. The film explores the first generation's confusion and ambivalence in respecting tradition and yet listening to their own needs and desires, the second generation's defiance of family impositions and desire to assimilate into British society, and the third generation's integration into British culture and ability to maneuver between the two cultures. In the film, the Saheli Asian Women's Center and its day trip are introduced not only as "female fun time" but most importantly as a shelter for South Asian women struggling to emancipate from patriarchal abuse and a vehicle for bridging the generational gap between first-generation immigrants, with their desire to maintain patriarchal traditions at the expense of female subjugation, and the U.K.-born younger generation, with their scorn for and rebellion against patriarchy and tradition. Although the trip is planned as an escape from their families and chaotic lives, their problems inevitably follow them, and the seaside trip becomes a "platform for their grievances to be heard and discussed" (Hussain 74).

The older women's traditional values—such as honor, duty, and sacrifice—along with their prejudices and racist attitudes against other ethnic groups, are introduced through a mix of comedic, dramatic, and fantastic scenes that evidence the racial and gender marginalization South Asians themselves experience in British society. For example, the film features waiters' whispered racist remarks in a coffee shop, a gang of hooligans' explicit racial insults, and drivers mocking the Saheli Asian Women's minibus on the highway. As was the case in *Inch'Allah* and *Flowers from Another World*, gender discrimination is also criticized in the film as an abusive pattern ingrained in a patriarchal culture where feminine subservience is the norm tolerated and perpetuated by female family members.

Two subplots constitute the dramatic core of the film and involve self-criticism of the Indian diaspora's racism and sexism. In one, Ginder, who has left her abusive husband, Ranjit, and taken their son Amrik with her to the shelter provided by the Saheli Asian Women's Center, is condemned by the older generation of Indian women for adopting "English" agency and independency and for destroying the "Indian" family (Hussain 75). The physical abuse to which Ginder has been subjected is ignored by older female family members and physical evidence is required for them to believe her testimonies: only after her bruises are exposed publicly at a male strippers' club they attend at the end of their trip do they start acknowledging the harm and take action to protect her (Desai 149). A related plot, the story of Hashida, who has been dating an African-Caribbean man, exposes the prejudices against Blacks within the South Asian community. Her relationship with Oliver also elicits reactionary responses from the older generation's women, especially after they discover her pregnancy, which reaffirms their view that contemporary England has contaminated Indian values and morals, providing only "social disharmony and religious decline" to their children and grandchildren (Hussain 78).

The positive outcome of the film shows the possibilities of gaining support and affirming solidarity through consciously belonging to and participating in a women's group. After their journey—which functions, following the convention of the road movie, as a budding and cathartic journey of self-discovery—the older South Asian women begin to understand their daughters' and granddaughters' plights; and Auntie Asha, who at the film's start was the most recalcitrant defender of patriarchal traditions, finds the strength to confront the abuser, and defend the victim of patriarchal abuse within her own family. Melodrama unfolds when at the end of their journey Ranjit, backed up by his brothers, finds Ginder in Blackpool and—after she refuses to return to him—insults her, beats her, and forcefully tries to kidnap their son Amrik. Patriarchy at its worst has been unveiled (Ginder's bruises) and is now staged in front of the women who need no more evidence to finally embrace Ginder's cause. Near the end of the film the women have witnessed the men's violence and sexist prejudices against women who "divorce" and have fun "without their husbands." Their unified final reaction is the plausible consequence of the budding relationships that have been established among them during their journey to the beach and prompted by Simi's feminist leadership.

The bus scenes during the round trip from Birmingham to Blackpool function as a structuring device to measure the process of the characters' feminist awareness. Before the journey starts, Simi addresses the "sisters" and states the Saheli Women's Center mission: "It is not often that we women get away from the patriarchal demands made on us by our daily lives, struggling between the double yoke of racism and sexism that we bear. This is your day. Have a female fun time." As Simi speaks, the camera fluctuates between the disapproving looks of older-generation Indian women and the cheerful screams of the younger U.K.-born girls, showing the existing generational gap with regard to women's attitudes toward patriarchy and racism, all of which will unfold in detail in the subsequent episodes they will run into while in Blackpool. In the closing scenes of the film, after Asha slaps Ranjit in the face calling him "brute and animal" and the younger brother rebels against his older brothers and helps the women to counteract their aggression, the women hop into the bus and pensively start their trip back home. The older women, who had shunned Ginder on their ride over and insulted Hashida while in Blackpool, now show Ginder their affection and support. As they pull out from Blackpool, Hashida greets them from her boyfriend's motorcycle and the older women acceptingly acknowledge her choice by saying, "[O]h, well; what can you do?" The journey has been cathartic for everyone and what prevails is the sense of female solidarity against male oppression. The journey's purpose and positive resolution are also highlighted by the musical soundtrack that accompanies the two scenes: a Punjabi rendition of the joyful Cliff Richard's classic, "Summer holiday" (1963), translated into Punjabi by Chadha herself and performed by the Bhangra band KK Kings.

As Jigna Desai argues, mobility and travel are significant to the agency of gendered diasporic subjects (135). Although their agency and mobility are accompanied by ambivalence, the films' characters resist power relations through seeking mobility away from abusive domestic spaces (136). Chadha utilizes the conventions of the road movie genre to better construct her immigrant characters' mobile, transitional, and transnational identities. In road movies, the road is in essence the passage to a new beginning, free from the bonds of the past, and potentially a journey of self-discovery. The road may also be a dead end that instead of conducing to utopia ends up in dystopia. Dangers and obstructions typically hinder the road to utopia, signifying that liberation from past and present constraints is not without complications, and creating the suspense that delays a successful conclusion. In a feminist variation of that pattern, Ginder and Hashida, who are hoping to escape albeit momentarily from their problems—domestic abuse and unwanted pregnancy—have to actively confront them while on the road. The road trip to Blackpool, as in most road movies, turns out to be not just a distraction but, on the contrary, a movable, unstable, and public arena where domestic and cultural patterns consubstantial to their gender roles in the diaspora unfold and ultimately get solved.

The cemetery scene in which Gregoria is finally convinced of her daughter-in-law's honest intentions (*Flowers*), and the public silencing of Zouina's main oppressor—her mother-in-law, Aïsha— effected by her husband and witnessed by the neighbors (*Inch'Allah*), present a characterization, narrative development, and positive resolution similar to the one introduced at the end of *Bhaji on the Beach*. The abuse and subjugation of immigrant women is affected by a patriarchal system based on tradition and supported by other women—who in the end understand their predicament through dialogue and shared experiences—and at the same time counteracted by a panoply of female immigrant and national characters who offered them their support from the start. The three films offer a multiplicity of female characters and are heterogeneous in their depiction of gendered migratory subjectivities.

European women filmmakers who tackle the subject of female immigration, regardless of nationality or ethnicity, share similar concerns and representation patterns: they emphasize female immigrants' agency, survival strategies and mechanisms of identity construction and integration into the receiving society over exit-less instances of subordination and domination. Their films may leave audiences with the impression that women filmmakers are prone to creating utopian narratives that offer change and hope rather than stagnation and despair. However utopian, their characters' growth is always contingent to the construction of affective links with other women, whether they are immigrant or natives, and the formation and upholding of female communities and associations. A general tendency among Western filmmakers who tackle the subject of immigration is to expose European countries' official and individual attitudes toward immigrants and critically examine the contradictions between reductive official immigration discourses and laws and immigrants' concrete experiences of urban life. Western European filmmakers' ethical commitments are in many cases less about the Other (the immigrant, the exploited), than they are about Europe's individual and institutional connivance with human rights abuses. (Ballesteros "Immigration Cinema" 197)

The daughters of immigrants themselves, Benguigui and Chadha focus on the issues that hindered the integration of newly arrived immigrant women to European societies. These are issues that originated equally in the host country's indifference or overt rejection and in the pressures migrant women are subjected to within the diaspora. Bollaín and Taberna, engaged white European intellectuals, position themselves with their immigrant subjects while critically contemplating the myriad attitudes their presence elicits in their European compatriots.[13] Intellectual and institutional awareness by European citizens about the prejudices and misconceptions that affect immigrants is an essential factor for positive change. What these women filmmakers add to the immigration genre is a gendered perspective that is still lacking in most media representations of female migration.

Notes

1. See my "Immigration Cinema in/and the European Union."
2. Referring to Latinas in the United States, Hondagneu-Sotelo points out that domestic work performed by immigrants "represents a bargain" for Western families and Western societies (24). The same thing can be stated about the lucrative businesses of mail-order brides, prostitution, and sex-slave rings, which would not be possible without the corruption of state officers, border and custom officials, and local law enforcement agencies, and the imposition of immigration laws that subject women to the control of agencies and rings, denying

them legal option and remedies, and reinforcing the immigrants' victimization by establishing the artificial distinction between "innocent victims" and "guilty sex workers" (Chapkis 929). See the articles by Christine Chun, Louise Shelley, and Wendy Chapkis.

3. Two examples of such tendency are *Lilya-4-Ever* (2003) by Lukas Moodysson and *Eastern Promises* (2007) by David Cronemberg.

4. Carpenter Latiri points out this connection: "Zouina's search will lead to her reunion/confrontation with Malika, her mirror and her antithesis" (my translation from French) (n.pag.).

5. Zouina's failure to establish a connection with her roots is symbolically enacted in her use of the headscarf to cover her self-inflicted wound. Zouina subverts the traditional Muslim custom of covering the head and puts the headscarf to good use, literally stopping the bleeding and symbolically signifying the suffering of these women. I thank Vilna Bashi Treitler for this interpretation.

6. The heavy past that haunts France and Algeria is symbolically buried when Zouina buries Madame Manant's dog. The friendship between Madame Manant, the widow of a French officer who died in Algeria, and Zouina is the optimistic representation of a sorority without resentment despite its colonial history (Carpenter Latiri; my translation from French).

7. The film fictionalizes an actual emergency solution devised by Spanish rural communities to reverse migration to the cities and revitalize the decreasing populations. The villages sponsor visits from single migrant women who can potentially become wives and save the family.

8. See the interview included in María Camí-Vela's book, *Mujeres detrás de la cámara* (2001).

9. On February 10, 2004, and after five months of intense public debate, the French General Assembly, following the recommendation of the Stasi commission, voted 494 to 36 to ban headscarves and all conspicuous religious signs, including Christian crosses and Jewish yarmulkes (Delphy 229). In 2002, Spain was also the epicenter of public controversy when Fatima Eldrisi, a 13-year-old Moroccan girl, was forbidden to wear the hijab while attending a public school. She was finally allowed to do so, which provided a significant victory for the Muslim community in Spain. For more information about the "battle of the hijab" (headscarf) in France and Spain, see articles by Christine Delphy and Parvati Nair.

10. I am borrowing the term used in Latin American Subaltern Studies to refer to a genre of literature that retells historical events from a subaltern's eyewitness perspective and uses strategies that describe the subject on its own terms instead of recasting it as the "Other" of the

dominant culture. Most "testimonies," prompted periods of social and political upheaval throughout Latin America, are based on traumatic sociopolitical episodes, convey a sense of orality, and are told from an individual perspective which nonetheless serves as an allegory for the communal experience as a whole. Some *testimonios*, such as Rigoberta Menchú's and Domitila Barrios's, are told by a person with limited literacy skills and transcribed by an intellectual or academic. See Ileana Rodríguez, ed., *The Latin American Subaltern Studies Reader.*

11. For previous close readings of the film see *Guía didáctica (Didactic Guide)* by Taberna and Costa-Villaverde and the articles "Embracing the Other" by Ballesteros and *Extranjeras* by Rodríguez. See also Rodríguez's "New Documentary Productions" for a nuanced application of Spivak's theories and analysis of the documentary genre.

12. Chadha is the first British South Asian woman to direct feature films. According to Yasmin Hussain, Chadha "occupies an important role as spokesperson for South Asian women as well as being in the position to challenge the misrepresentations of South Asian women within mainstream film" (71). Her documentary for the BBC *I Am English But . . .* (1989) and her most recent and commercially successful *Bend It Like Beckham* (2002) also explore generational differences between young British South Asians and their parents.

13. For an introduction to the genre's conventions, see David Laderman's book *Driving Visions. Exploring the Road Movie.*

Works Cited

Ballesteros, Isolina. "Embracing the Other: The Feminization of Spanish 'Immigration Cinema.'" *Studies in Hispanic Cinemas* 2.1 (2005): 3–14. Print.

———. "Immigration Cinema in/and the European Union." *Cultural and Media Studies. European Perspectives.* Ed. María Pilar Rodríguez. Vol. 1. Reno: U of Nevada P, 2009. 189–215. Print.

Bauman, Zygmunt. "Making and Unmaking of Strangers." *Stranger or Guest? Racism and Nationalism in Contemporary Europe.* Ed. Sandro Fridlizius and Abby Paterson. Stockholm: Göteburg U, 1996. 59–79. Print.

Ben Jelloun, Tahar. *French Hospitality: Racism and North African Immigrants.* Trans. Barbara Bray. New York: Columbia UP, 1999. Print.

Braziel, Jana Evans, and Anita Mannur, eds. *Theorizing Diaspora. A Reader.* Oxford: Blackwell, 2003. Print.

Camí-Vela, María. *Mujeres detrás de la cámara. Entrevistas con cineastas españolas de la década de los 90.* Madrid: Ocho y Medio, 2001. Print.

————. "Entrevista con Helena Taberna (Madrid: enero 2004)." *Guía didáctica: Extranjeras. Una película documental de Helena Taberna.* Ed. Helena Taberna and Elisa Costa-Villaverde. Pamplona: Lamia Producciones Audiovisuales S. L., 2005. 48–53. Print.

Carpenter Latiri, Dora. "Représentations de la femme migrante dans *Inch'Allah dimanche.*" Web. <http://wjfms.ncl.ac.uk/LatiriWJ.htm>.

Chapkis, Wendy. "Trafficking, Migration, and the Law: Protecting Innocents, Punishing Immigrants." *Gender and Society* 17. 6 (Dec. 2003): 923–37. Print.

Chun, Christine. "The Mail-Order Bride Industry: The Perpetuation of Transnational Economic Inequalities and Stereotypes." *University of Pennsylvania Journal of International Economic Law* 17.4 (Winter 1996): 1155–1208. Print.

Delphy, Christine. "Gender, Race and Racism: The Ban of the Islamic Headscarf in France." *Transnational Migration and the Politics of Identity.* Ed. Meenakshi Thapan. New Delhi: Sage, 2005. 228–51. Print.

Desai, Jigna. "Homesickness and Motion Sickness: Embodied Migratory Subjectivities in Gurinder Chadha's *Bhaji on the Beach.*" *Beyond Bollywood: The Cultural Politics of South Asian Diasporic Film.* New York: Routledge, 2004. 133–58. Print.

Dijk, Teun A. van. "Nuevo racismo y noticias. Un enfoque discursivo." *Inmigración, género y espacios urbanos. Los retos de la diversidad.* Ed. Mary Nash, Rosa Tello, and Núria Benach. Barcelona: Edicions Bellaterra, 2005. 33–55. Print.

Fauvel, Maryse. "Yamina Benguigui's *Inch'Allah dimanche*: Unveiling Hybrid Identities." *Studies in French Cinema* 4.2 (2004): 147–57. Print.

García Armand, Asun. "El rol de las mujeres en el devenir de un barrio intercultural: El Raval de Barcelona." *Inmigración, género y espacios urbanos. Los retos de la diversidad.* Ed. Mary Nash, Rosa Tello, and Núria Benach. Barcelona: Edicions Bellaterra, 2005. 123–40. Print.

Hondagneu-Sotelo, Pierrette. "New World Domestic Order." *Domestica.* Berkeley: U of California P, 2007. 3–28. Print.

Hussain, Yasmin. "*Bhaji on the Beach* and *Bend It like Beckham*: Gurinder Chadha and the 'Desification' of British Cinema." *Writing Diaspora. South Asian Women, Culture and Ethnicity.* Hampshire: Ashgate, 2005. 71–90. Print.

Juliano, Dolores. "La reconstrucción de la identidad a partir de sus límites." *Intersticios. Contactos interculturales, género y dinámicas identitarias en Barcelona.* Ed. Rosa Tello, Núria Benach, and Mary Nash. Barcelona: Edicions Bellaterra, 2008. 193–223. Print.

Kofman, Eleonore. "Female 'Birds of Passage' a Decade Later: Gender and Immigration in the European Union." *International Migration Review* 33.2 (Summer 1999): 269–99. Print.

Laderman, David. *Driving Visions. Exploring the Road Movie.* Austin: U of Texas P, 2002. Print.

Morokvasic, Mirjana. "Birds of Passage are also Women . . ." *International Migration Review* 18.4 (Winter 1984): 886–907. Print.

Nair, Parvati. "Moor-Veiled Matters: The Hijab as Troubling Interrogative of the Relation between the West and Islam." *New Formations* 51 (Winter 2003–2004): 39–49. Print.

Nash, Mary. "La doble alteridad en la comunidad imaginada de las mujeres inmigrantes." *Inmigración, género y espacios urbanos. Los retos de la diversidad.* Ed. Mary Nash, Rosa Tello, and Núria Benach. Barcelona: Edicions Bellaterra, 2005. 17–31.Print.

Pérez-Rincón, Socorro, and Asun García Armand. "Estrategias identitarias en los espacios de contacto." *Intersticios. Contactos interculturales, género y dinámicas identitarias en Barcelona.* Ed. Rosa Tello, Núria Benach, and Mary Nash. Barcelona: Edicions Bellaterra, 2008. 100–145. Print.

Raijman, Rebeca, Silvina Schammah-Gesser, and Adriana Kemp. "International Migration, Domestic Work, and Care Work: Undocumented Latina Migrants in Israel." *Gender and Society* 17.5 (Oct. 2003): 727–49. Print.

Rodríguez, Ileana, ed. *The Latin American Subaltern Studies Reader.* Durham: Duke UP, 2001. Print.

Rodríguez, María Pilar. *Extranjeras: Migraciones, globalización, multiculturalismo.* Vitoria: Arabako Foru Alduncia and Diputación Floral de Álava, 2005. Print.

———. "New Documentary Productions: A New Speaking Position for Migrant Subjects in *Extranjeras* and *Si nos dejan.*" *Catalan Journal of Communication and Cultural Studies* 2.1 (2010): 43–58. Print.

Shelley, Louise. "Trafficking in Women: The Business Model Approach." *Brown Journal of World Affairs* 10.1 (Summer/Fall 2003): 119–31. Print.

Shohat, Ella. "Post-Third-Worldist Culture. Gender, Nation and the Cinema." *Rethinking Third Cinema.* Ed. Anthony R. Gutneratne and Wimal Dissanayake. New York: Routledge, 2003. 51–78. Print.

Solé, Carlota, and Sonia Parella. "Migrant Women in Spain: Class, Gender and Ethnicity." *Gender and Ethnicity in Contemporary Europe.* Ed. Jacqueline Andall. Oxford: Berg, 2003. 61–76. Print.

Spivak, Gayatri. "Can the Subaltern Speak?" *Imperialism. Critical Concepts in Historical Studies.* Ed. Peter Cain and Mark Harrison. London: Routledge, 2001. 171–219. Print.

Taberna, Helena, and Elisa Costa-Villaverde. *Guía didáctica:* Extranjeras. *Una película documental de Helena Taberna.* Pamplona: Lamia Producciones Audiovisuales S. L., 2005.

Tello i Robira, Rosa. "Espacios urbanos y zonas de contacto intercultural." *Inmigración, género y espacios urbanos. Los retos de la diversidad.* Ed.

Mary Nash, Rosa Tello, and Núria Benach. Barcelona: Edicions Bellaterra, 2005. 85–97. Print.

Thapan, Meenakshi, ed. "Introduction: 'Making Incomplete': Identity, Woman and the Politics of Identity." *Transnational Migration and the Politics of Identity*. New Delhi: Sage, 2005. 23–62. Print.

Zontini, Elisabetta. "Migraciones, género y multiculturalismo. Una perspectiva de Europa meridional." *Inmigración, género y espacios urbanos. Los retos de la diversidad*. Ed. Mary Nash, Rosa Tello, and Núria Benach. Barcelona: Edicions Bellaterra, 2005. 99–122. Print.

Conclusion

Gesa Zinn and Maureen Tobin Stanley

The authors of the chapters in this book have identified and discussed women's exilic existences and alienhood in history, literature, and film within Europe's open borders and boundaries. As exile experiences are unique and universal, it is impossible to represent them all. We as editors have thus chosen to provide a glimpse of gendered views revealed to us from their "otherness," their alienhood, their alienation, and their reality of exilic living. Within the English-, French-, German-, and Spanish-speaking world and within a variety of settings during different time periods, we as authors have confronted and explored what Julia Kristeva terms "the foreigner within ourselves" through the experience of transience and foreignness. Readers will find that each chapter builds on the previous one. For example, in Chapter 1, by Paula Hanssen, we have chosen Elisabeth Hauptmann and Margarete Steffin to be the first women in our text whose lives allow readers a glimpse into the restless, energetic, tireless, and yet often lonely and alienated world of writing, collaboration, and survival. In the second chapter, by Mary Thrond, the world of María Teresa León shows some similarities to that of Hauptmann and Steffin. She also wrote and stood in the shadow of a male companion and fellow writer. But motherhood, along with León's melancholia, adds an additional layer of pain and alienation, underlining the very personal and often intricate circumstances that distance exiled women from others in exile. This point, written between the lines, is made throughout the readings. We would like to call attention to the reality that women in exile share characteristics of "female exile living," even though their circumstances—and their experience of these circumstances—are unique. Paradoxically, the condition of double marginality and alienation, bound together with that of exile, unifies and universalizes women's exilic experiences.

An example of this universality is also portrayed in Chapter 3, by Kimberle López. In Alicia Dujovne Ortiz's novel, the protagonist-narrator's daughter, who is from Buenos Aires, lives in France. Her exile is construed as a type of imprisonment from which she likely cannot be liberated. Her choice is to stay in France or to find another place of exile. But her desire cannot be fulfilled simply by changing venues. She can only escape her exilic, physical imprisonment by constructing an imaginary homeland. For Adelheid Eubanks, the author of the next chapter, and for the protagonist in Christa Wolf's novel *Medea*, the situation is similar. Their shared home country ceases to exist as do many of its values and ideals, and as do the past lives of the two women. The question(ing) of identity, which continually occupies the exile's mind, as seen in Chapter 3, functions on three levels in Chapter 4—namely, that of the author, the protagonist, and the state of East Germany, which after forty years ceased to exist in 1990 when East and West Germany were reunified. The problem of identity and identification with the old and the new, the past and the present, and the personal (author and protagonist) and the public (society and the state) as a multifaceted concept within women's exile living comes to the foreground particularly in Chapters 3 and 4.

Maureen Tobin Stanley's chapter, Chapter 5, picks up where Eubanks's leaves off; for here we have in Icíar Bollaín's film text a protagonist who, not unlike the ones in the two preceding chapters, has no sense of home or belonging. Married to an abusive husband, she had adopted his view of her as marginal, as "Other," as banished. Her recourse is to see "home" within a psychic landscape. She discovers the world of symbology (art and mythology), and thus escapes exile by creating a new home within herself, by seeing herself with new eyes, and liberating herself from patriarchal myths of female banishment. Thus she goes beyond confronting Kristeva's foreigner within and the pain of everyday life. Chapter 6, by Gesa Zinn, like the previous chapter, deals with this pain and the different stages of identity construction. In Fatih Akin's film text more than one character struggles with belonging as it relates to identity, each in her own way and within her own circumstances and geographical places. What we see here are not only attempts to cope with the pain of structuring and reconfiguring old and new identities but also bimodal skewings of exilic experiences along gender lines. In other words, Akin's male characters are not successful in de-alienating the foreigner within, whereas the female characters are. Because of their adaptability to new surroundings and the relative ease of establishing social connections, the women, unlike the men, experience a livable exile.

The final chapter, Chapter 7, is by Isolina Ballesteros. Viewed as a culmination of this anthology, it shows the manner in which some women exiles creatively see a way out of apparently "no-exit" situations that are frequently part of exile living. Ballesteros takes a serious look at individual women on the screen who come to see their authentic selves and ultimately triumph. The works studied in this final chapter present the reader with a clear picture of the resilience of groups of women who refuse to accept the limitations and imposed marginalization of heteronomously perceived alienhood. Moreover, Ballesteros classifies a particular genre, namely, female immigration films made by women, which gives its subjects a voice that is often at odds with the general assumption about female immigration. Furthermore, as Ballesteros claims, female immigration cinema by women is driven by a common desire to undo female migrants' invisibility and foster the creation of sociality and solidarity among women exiles. All in all then, in reading these chapters in order, the reader steps into the thick of female exilic experiences. It is our hope that this compendium sheds light on ways in which the woman exile can live in relative peace, after having confronted the foreigner within and after having constructed a new vision of her new identity.

In conclusion, through our selection of essays about exiled women in history, literature, fiction, and film within the European context of the twentieth and twenty-first centuries' transnational and migration movements, we as editors have striven to provide our readers with a window into women's exilic existences and alienhood. While each chapter of *Exile Through a Gendered Lens: Women's Displacement in Recent European History, Literature and Film* can be read on its own terms, each is also part of a whole, namely, a presentation of the unfolding layers of the portrayal of a woman's exilic existence. From the individual to the more common "group" experiences, alienation, identity, and the foreign are concepts with which all the women (both factual and fictional) discussed in this book grapple.

The female figures studied, within the context of this volume, go from the marginalized subjectivity of Brecht's collaborators Steffin and Hauptmann, Spanish exile María Teresa León, inner exile Wolf, and displaced person Dujovne Ortiz, to the alienated objectification visible in Akin's and Bollaín's films. An overarching, unifying characteristic of the women is their shared point of departure: projected alienhood or foreignness internalized and expressed subjectively through the gendered lens of "otherness." On the other hand, the progression, evolution, and result of how each fictitious and factual woman sees herself differ. Whereas Hauptmann and Steffin could not overcome the foreigner within, León's and Dujovne Ortiz's process—almost a quixotic fight—can be regarded in a positive light. The films of Bollaín, Benguigui, Taberna, Chadha, and Akin portray transformative experiences, as the female characters desist in seeing themselves as aliens, foreigners, or marginalized others. Through their newly formulated self-perceptions they regain subjective authenticity, seeing themselves for who they are, who they aim to be, not how others view them. Hence marginality and "otherness" (as imposed by heteronomous vantage points) are transformed and subverted as autonomous characters come to see themselves. Ways of seeing tend to reflect an outlook on life, but a way of regarding the self reveals not an outlook but perhaps an "inlook;" such is the focus of the works studied in this volume. By validating their inherent identities—not the external markers such as place of origin—the women and characters in the works studied here underscore their value as women and human beings. Although physically displaced, those who are victorious are rooted in a sense of self, a knowledge that home connotes seeing themselves as they are wherever they might be.

To see is to apply meaning, to understand, but also to identify with those whose views are visible to the seer. In this light, we hope that the readers of our book will be able to see the multiple exilic experiences that have been presented through a wide, gendered lens. In so doing, perhaps the reader can face, embrace, and ultimately de-alienate the foreigner within.

Notes on Contributors

Isolina Ballesteros is an associate professor in the Department of Modern Languages and Comparative Literature and the Film Studies Program of Baruch College, the City University of New York. She is the author of two books: *Escritura femenina y discurso autobiográfico en la nueva novela española* (New York, 1994) and *Cine (Ins) urgente: textos fílmicos y contextos culturales de la España posfranquista* (Madrid, 2001). She is currently working on a book titled *(Un)desirable Otherness and (Im)migration Cinema in the European Union.*

Adelheid Eubanks (MA, Washington University—St. Louis; PhD, Johnson C. Smith University) is a native of Cologne, Germany, and a professor in the Modern Language and Literatures Department at Johnson C. Smith University in Charlotte, North Carolina. Her research interests include narrative and European cultural identity.

Paula Hanssen (PhD, University of Illinois–Urbana) is the chair of International Languages and Cultures and coordinator of German Studies at Webster University in St. Louis, Missouri. Her publications include *Elisabeth Hauptmann: Brecht's Silent Collaborator*, as well as articles on Brecht's female collaborators.

Kimberle S. **López** is an associate professor of Latin American literature in the Department of Spanish and Portuguese at the University of New Mexico. In 2002, she published *Latin American Novels of the Conquest: Reinventing the New World*, which examines the representation of colonial desire in a corpus of recent Latin American historical fictions that rewrite the chronicles of the conquest and colonization of the Americas. Her recent research focuses on themes such as the relationships among migration, exile, and diaspora; ethnography, history, and fiction; and cannibalism, colonialism, and commodity fetishism.

Mary Thrond (MA, University of Salamanca, 2004) has worked as a world languages program consultant in Europe, Asia, South America, and the United States and is a frequent presenter at local, regional, and national conferences. She has taught collegiate-level Spanish in New York City and Minnesota as well as English as a Foreign Language (EFL) in Spain. She directed the language immersion program at Concordia Language Villages. After studying linguistic anthropology at the University of Wisconsin–Madison, she spent nearly a decade teaching EFL and directing an educational exchange program in Madrid.

Maureen Tobin Stanley (PhD, Michigan State University, 2000) is an associate professor at the University of Minnesota–Duluth. Tobin Stanley has published articles on Spanish female authors, cinema, exile, and deportation. Her books include *Female Exiles in 20th and 21st Century Europe* (New York, 2007; coedited by Gesa Zinn), *Hybridity in Spanish Culture* (New Castle upon Tyne, 2010; coedited by Tajes and Knudson-Vilaseca), and *Voces e imágenes del Holocausto en la cultura española* (currently under review).

Gesa Zinn (PhD, University of Minnesota, 1995) is an associate professor of German studies in the Department of Foreign Languages and Literatures at the University of Minnesota–Duluth. She has published articles on pedagogy and German culture, film, and literature and is the coeditor (with Maureen Tobin Stanley) of *Female Exiles in 20th and 21st Century Europe* (New York, 2007). Her recent research focuses on issues of gender, exile, transnationalism, identity, and human trafficking. Zinn's current book project is titled *Female, Urban and Exiled: Gypsies in 21st Century Germany.*

Index